THE AIRBNB PLAYBOOK

THE AIRBNB PLAYBOOK

Your Complete Guide to Start and Manage a
Profitable Airbnb Business

JAMES STEWARD

Copyright © 2019 - All rights reserved.

No part of this book or any portion thereof may be reproduced or transmitted in any form or by any means, electronic or mechanical, including photocopying, recording, or by any information storage and retrieval system without the written permission of the author or publisher.

Under no circumstances will any blame or legal responsibility be held against the publisher, or author for any damages, reparation, or monetary loss due to the information contained within this book. Either directly or indirectly.

Legal Notice

This book is copyright protected. This book is only for personal use. You cannot amend, distribute, sell, use, quote or paraphrase any part, or content within this book, without the consent of the author or publisher.

Disclaimer Notice

Please note that the information contained within this document is for educational and entertainment purposes only. All effort has been executed to present accurate, up to date, and reliable, complete information. No warranties of any kind are declared or implied. Readers acknowledge that the author is not engaging in the rendering of legal, financial, medical, or professional advice. The content in this book has been derived from various sources. Please consult a licensed professional before attempting any techniques outlined in this book.

By reading this document, the reader agrees that under no circumstances is the author responsible for any losses, direct or indirect, which are incurred as a result of the use of information contained within this document, including, but not limited to, errors, omissions, or inaccuracies.

BONUS CONTENT!!

As a thank you for putting your trust in me and this book I am giving every reader free access to download all the free tools and templates me and my team have created and that helped us succeed on our Airbnb journey.

You can download all the tools and templates here:

www.theairbnbplaybook.com/tools

Please keep this link private and do not redistribute it.
Thank you

James

CONTENT

Introduction 1

Chapter 1: What is Airbnb? 6
How did Airbnb start? 7
How does it work? 9
Is it safe? 10
How can I make money from Airbnb? 10
Why use Airbnb? 11

Chapter 2: Before You Start - Planning 12
Things to consider before you begin 13
Generating income and achieving financial freedom 15
The three options 17
Market and Area research 18
Competition analysis in your area 23
How much money will your property generate as an Airbnb rental? 24
Safety and Security 30
Is Airbnb is regulated in your area? 33
Business type and taxes 36
Chapter 2 Key Points 38

Chapter 3: Getting Ready to Start - Preparation 40
You already own a property you want to list on Airbnb 41
You already rent a property you want to list on Airbnb 42
Renting a property to list on Airbnb 42
Buying a property to list on Airbnb 45
Putting it all together 47

Maintaining your property 49

Chapter 3 Key Points 51

Chapter 4: Preparing your property 52

Must-have features 53

Furnishing, Decorating and Equipping your Airbnb rental property 53

Chapter 4 Key Points 64

Chapter 5: Listing your property 66

Overview of the Airbnb listing process 67

Instant Book, One Night Minimum and Additional Guests 75

Airbnb Host Status 78

Tips to make your listing stand out 82

Earth Friendly Airbnb 82

Advertising your property on other platforms 83

SEO for your Airbnb listing 84

Google Adwords 85

Using local travel and booking sites 86

Chapter 5 Key Points 87

Chapter 6: Running the Property 88

Receiving bookings and communications 89

Preparing for Guests to arrive 90

Welcoming Guests 92

Dealing with issues during guest stays and communications during their stay 93

How to deal with guests who won't leave 95

The Check-out process 96

The Airbnb Review Process 96

5 Star Review Checklist 100

Chapter 6 Key Points 104

Chapter 7: Cleaning and reset 106

    Doing it yourself or getting help? 107

    Cleaning and re-set Checklist 109

    How long will cleaning take? 110

    Using a Property Management Service? 111

    Chapter 7 Key Points 114

Chapter 8: Useful tools and Bonus Content 116

    Contacting Airbnb 117

    Useful Links 118

    Useful Tools 119

    How to write a great guest review 120

    How to improve your guests' experience 121

    Slow season strategies 122

    Create Additional Revenue Streams 124

    Automating your Airbnb Business 125

Conclusion 131

Glossary 133

Index of Links 134

Index 136

INTRODUCTION

Are you looking to start a business on the side to earn some extra income? Perhaps you want to grow this business to become financially independent and free up your time to travel or do what you love?

Well, why not become an Airbnb entrepreneur?

Airbnb is a global community for hosts and travelers with over six million listings in more than eighty thousand cities covering one hundred and ninety countries worldwide. On average, more than two million people stay in Airbnb accommodation every night of the year.

Initially, Airbnb provided an opportunity for hosts to rent out vacant space in a property and to make a little money on the side. It has allowed some people to quit their jobs to become full-time Airbnb hosts and achieve **financial freedom, even if you have little or no startup capital!**

Whether you want to make a little additional revenue or if you want to generate a primary revenue stream through Airbnb, there are essential things you need to know to get started and common pitfalls and mistakes you want to avoid to reach your goals efficiently and effectively.

That's what this book is all about. I will lay out everything you need to know to become a successful Airbnb host and to make money from the global Airbnb community.

THE AIRBNB PLAYBOOK

Let's take a quick look at what topics the book will cover and how it will set you on your path to success:

- **Planning** – Many new Airbnb hosts fail because they jump in without planning – this section will cover everything you need to know before you start. Market and research, target demographics, finding a property, buying or renting, and tools to help you do it all.

- **Preparation** – Setting up your property, Insurance, finances, and the must-have features, appliances, and gadgets your guests demand and will get you a 5-star rating.

- **Listing** – How to create an eye-catching listing on Airbnb that will trump the competition and generate bookings.

- **Running your Airbnb property** – Dealing with day to day aspects, guests, cleaning and reset after quests and the Airbnb review process.

- **Bonus content** – Useful tools and links to help you get started and pro tips on automating the Airbnb process as well as slow season strategies to boost revenue.

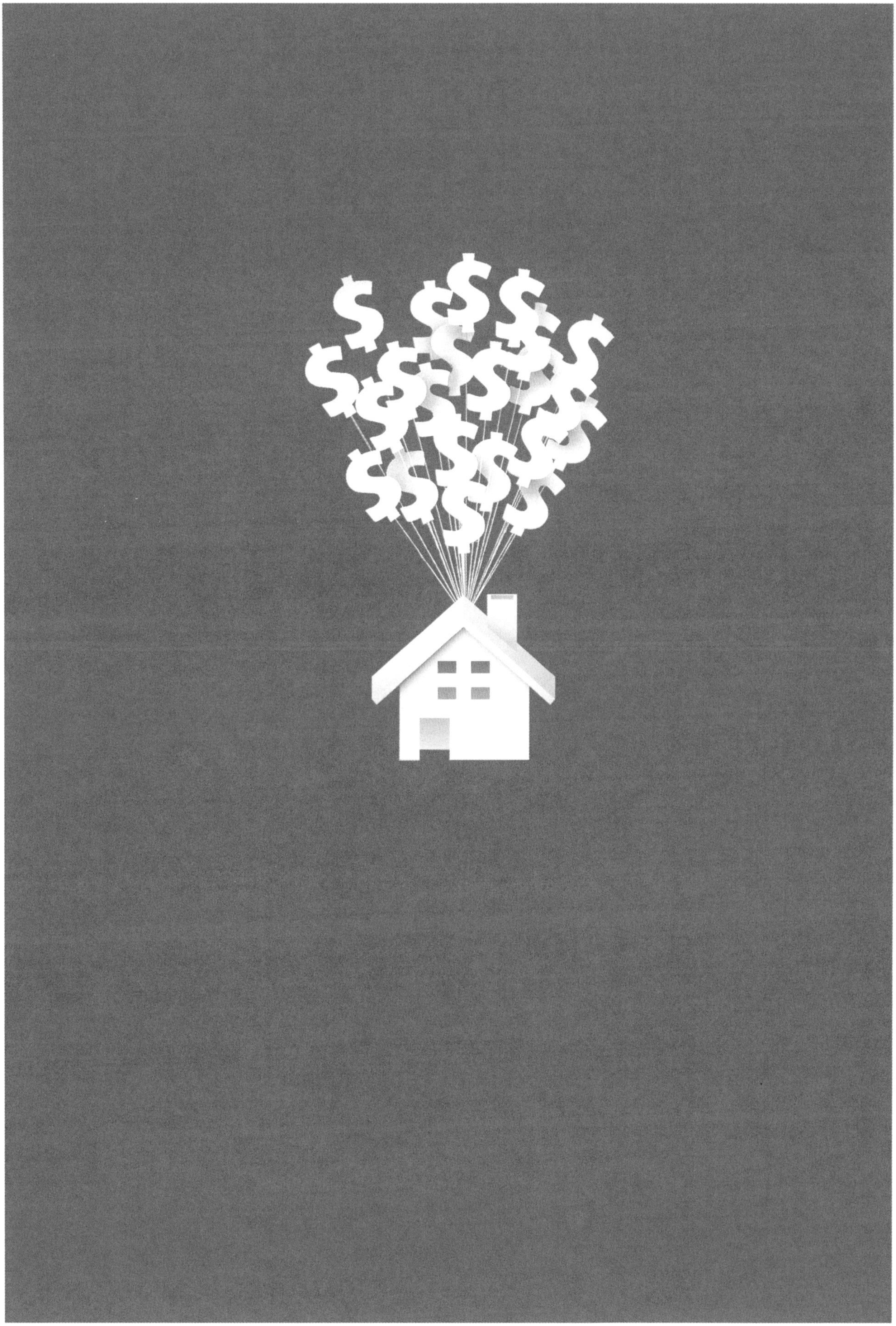

NOTE FROM
THE AUTHOR

My name is James Stewart, and I have become a successful Airbnb entrepreneur over the last five years and own twelve properties outright that are currently being rented on Airbnb and a further five properties that I have listed via rental arbitrage.

Starting an Airbnb business has been very rewarding both from a personal growth and financial perspective.

I have created this book with two other Airbnb entrepreneurs that have had similar success with Airbnb, to help and guide other people that are interested in achieving financial freedom through Airbnb hosting and teach you how to emulate our success.

I hope you find the information in this book helpful and that it will accelerate your path to success.

All the best

James Steward

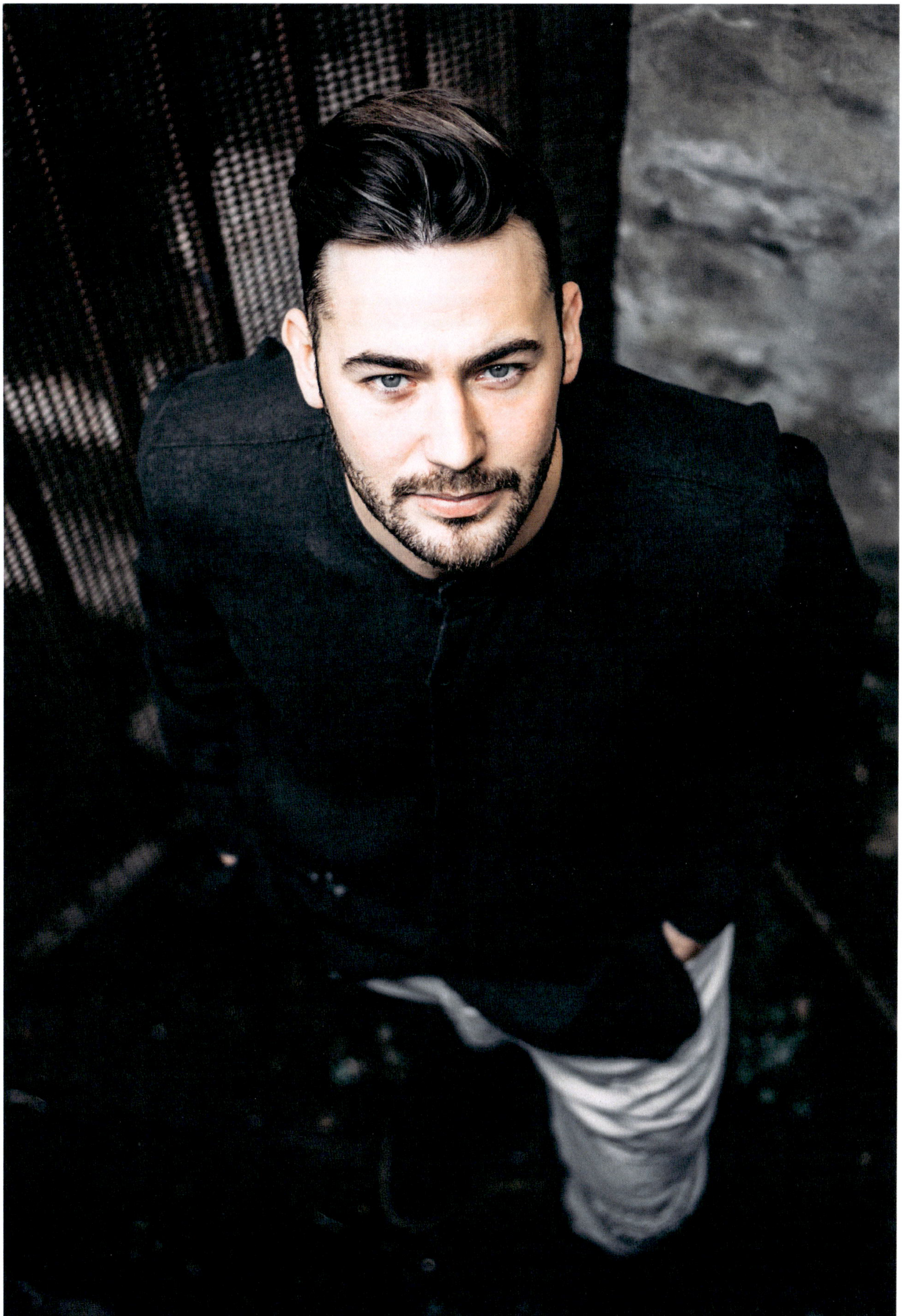

1

WHAT IS AIRBNB?

1. What is Airbnb?

HOW DID AIRBNB START?

In October 2007, two young men from New York were having problems paying the rent on their shared apartment in San Francisco. Neither Brian Chesky nor Joe Gebbia had been able to find work and, their rent had suddenly increased by twenty-five percent.

However, they noticed that virtually all the hotels in the city were fully booked due to the IDSA Industrial Design conference. Why not, they thought, offer people the opportunity to sleep on an inflatable mattress on the floor in their apartment to bring in a little extra cash? They created a web site, Air Mattress Bed and Breakfast, and offered people the opportunity to spend the night on an airbed for $80. Three people responded and became the very first Airbnb guests.

Soon after, Harvard graduate and technical architect Nathan Blecharczyk joined Chesky and Gebbia and in March 2008 during the South by Southwest Music Conference and Festival (SXSW) in Texas, Airbed and Breakfast was officially launched. It attracted a total of two bookings.

In August 2008 the Airbed and Breakfast website was launched in time for the Democratic Conference in Denver. It attracted eighty bookings. In March 2009 the venture was renamed Airbnb and expanded from covering just rooms to include apartments, houses and even vacation rentals. Interest in the concept of Airbnb snowballed in the US and by 2013 the company made the first move towards international operations with the opening of an office in Germany.

THE AIRBNB PLAYBOOK

Joe Gebbia, Nathan Blecharczyk and Brian Chesky
Image; Airbnb Media Resources

In 2014, Airbnb listings attracted more than one hundred thousand guests during the Soccer World Cup in Rio de Janeiro. In 2015, Airbnb became the official alternative accommodation services supplier for the Olympic Games which were also held in Rio in 2016. The company became so successful that later that year, the White House appointed Brian Chesky *Presidential Ambassador for Global Entrepreneurship.*

Airbnb is currently the largest property sharing site and has a net worth of over $25 billion. The company employs more than three thousand people and is still run by Brian Chesky, Joe Gebbia, and Nathan Blecharczyk.

Airbnb is an important element of what has become known as *the sharing economy* – using the Internet as the primary means of connecting sellers and consumers to sell or rent services or underutilized assets.

1. What is Airbnb?

Airbnb HQ
Image; Airbnb Media Resources

HOW DOES IT WORK?

Airbnb provides an online marketplace where hosts can list properties for rent. These listings include photographs of the property, location information, details of the accommodation and facilities, and reviews from previous guests. Guests can search listings using a number of criteria.

Hosts don't pay for listing their property, but Airbnb retains around 3% of the cost of each booking from hosts in commission and up to 20% from guests. Guests pay in full, in advance through a secure platform and hosts receive payment twenty-four hours after their guests check-in. Airbnb provides a 24-hour support and assistance hotline for both hosts and guests.

IS IT SAFE?

Airbnb provides several mechanisms for ensuring the safety and security of both hosts and guests. Before enrolling a host or guest in the system, Airbnb verifies their identity by using social media and scanned documents. In some locations and in specific circumstances (last-minute bookings, for example) Airbnb requires the submission of a scanned photo ID such as a driver's license or passport.

However, the most notable way of evaluating potential hosts or guests is the peer-to-peer review system which allows both host and guests to leave reviews. Reviews can only be left after a reservation has been completed. In general, Airbnb will not remove reviews unless they violate the company content policy (by providing personally identifying information about a host or guest, for example) but they will allow a response to a negative review. Reviews are the main way in which guests assess potential hosts and vice-versa.

HOW CAN I MAKE MONEY FROM AIRBNB?

Your home is an asset, but it may be underutilized in terms of generating income. You may want to bring in a little extra cash by renting out space in your home on Airbnb from time to time. You may have more ambitious plans that involve renting or buying a property specifically to list on Airbnb.

Whatever approach you will take, to assess how much money you can make on Airbnb you need to be able to calculate your expenses and your potential income. The Planning Chapter provides all the information you need to calculate both, enabling you to predict your potential Airbnb profit.

1. What is Airbnb?

WHY USE AIRBNB?

Airbnb currently has the biggest slice of the short-term, property sharing rental market and the Airbnb brand has become globally recognized. If you are a host, you currently have access to more potential guests through Airbnb than if you use any other system. That's an important consideration if you aim to make money out of rentals.

However, there are alternatives. Mainstream Internet accommodation booking services such as Agoda and Booking.com now offer space in homes or rentals of privately-owned property in addition to professionally operated hotels and guesthouses. Specialist services like VRBO (Vacation Rentals By Owner) cover rentals for extended periods in accommodation suited to families or groups.

It is important to decide if Airbnb is right for you. If you own a large, beachside property which you want to rent out only during the summer months, perhaps a specialist service like VRBO might be best? If you have a city apartment and you're happy to take short-term rentals, Airbnb may be the best choice. Do your research and decide if Airbnb is right for you.

This book is mainly aimed at people who choose to become Airbnb hosts, though much of the advice and guidance provided here is also applicable to hosts who use other listing services.

2

BEFORE YOU START:
PLANNING

2. Before You Start - Planning

THINGS TO CONSIDER BEFORE YOU BEGIN

One of the most common mistakes that beginner Airbnb hosts make is to fail to plan properly. Remember the business adage: *Failing to Plan is Planning to Fail!* That is as true for setting up an Airbnb business as it is for any other and this Chapter will help you to plan effectively.

SET GOALS BUT BE REALISTIC!

Before you begin, you need to be clear about your goals for becoming an Airbnb host. This book will give you the tools to understand what you need to do to be successful, but you must be realistic about what you can actually achieve. Do you hope to make a little extra cash from time to time? Do you plan to establish a stable secondary income flow? Do you intend to create an Airbnb business that will become your main source of income?

All three are possible depending on the amount of time you have to invest, the property you have or that you intend to rent or buy and the accommodation market in the area. Of course, you can start small and build up later, but it is important that you are clear about what your immediate, short-term and long-term goals are.

Take some time to think about what you want to get out of your Airbnb hosting now, in six months' time and in one year and in two years. Setting this type of goal is an important part of establishing any successful business.

TIME CONSTRAINTS

Becoming an Airbnb host will take time to plan, to prepare your property and to create an effective and engaging listing. When your property is listed you will need time to meet with your guests, to deal with any issues they may have and to prepare the property for the next guests. You may see Airbnb described in some places as a way of generating passive income, but this is misleading – you need to put in time and effort to become a successful Airbnb host.

You can automate some of the work and you can sub-contract some things to specialist services, but that will cut into your revenue. In general terms, the more income potential you want to realize, the more time you are going to have to put in to achieve your goals. How much time do you have? Is this something you plan to do in your spare time or will it become your main occupation? Be realistic about this too and don't underestimate the amount of time required – many beginner Airbnb hosts are shocked by how much time it takes.

> *Pro-Tip: Running an Airbnb property will almost certainly take longer than you imagine – don't underestimate this when you are planning.*

RESEARCH AND UNDERSTAND THE MARKET

Effective research is essential to starting any new business. You need to understand the market in your area, especially in terms of accommodation supply and demand. You also need to identify the target demographic for your guests. You can do this yourself but there are tools available which can help, and these are discussed in more detail later in this book.

DEALING WITH PEOPLE AND STRANGERS

When you become an Airbnb host, you are effectively becoming part of the hospitality industry. This requires fundamental people skills – the ability to communicate effectively with guests both face-to-face and using messaging. Do you have these skills? Do you have personal, language, writing or other issues that may impact your ability to communicate effectively with guests? What can you do to address these issues? Can you sub-contract the things that you find challenging? Will your Airbnb rental still be commercially viable if you do this?

Assessing your own people skills can be difficult – try telling people who know you well that you are considering becoming an Airbnb host and gauge their reactions. If they are skeptical, stunned or even horrified, find out why. Can you address the issues they raise? You need to think these things through objectively and realistically before you decide to become an Airbnb host.

2. Before You Start - Planning

GENERATING INCOME AND ACHIEVING FINANCIAL FREEDOM

People become Airbnb hosts in order to make money, but just how much can you make? An essential part of understanding this is to create a Business Plan.

YOUR BUSINESS PLAN

Every new business needs a Business Plan. There are two reasons for this; first, it forces you to think in detail about the new business which is a good way of avoiding potential failures or problems. Second, having a good Business Plan allows you to share your vision with others. That's essential if you are considering looking for financing or any other form of professional assistance.

You will find lots of publications and web sites that provide good advice on producing an effective Business Plan, but in simple terms, the plan must provide the reader with the answers to the five essential questions; *How?, What?, When?, Where?,* and *Why?*

As a minimum, your Business Plan should set out;

- An overview of how you intend to make money from Airbnb including which property you will be using or in which areas you want to find properties for sale or rent. This should include a summary of the data obtained during your research into both demand and competition in the area. This part should also show that you understand the regulatory requirements for Airbnb hosts in your area and describe how you will comply with them as well as demonstrating that you will have appropriate insurance.

- A financial plan showing how much you believe you can make through Airbnb (including the research and data that led you to this conclusion) balanced against your time and property costs. The details here will depend on whether you already own or rent the property or if you are planning to rent or purchase a property specifically to list on Airbnb – more detail on these options is provided in the next sections.

- Any potential problems or pitfalls that you anticipate and how you will deal with them. Think here about potential changes in your personal circumstance, changes in the accommodation market or the level of competition as well as possible regulatory changes.

- A vision of when you intend to start the business and where you expect it to be in six months, one year and two years.

- Introduce the whole thing with an Executive Summary which condenses all the essential information to answer those five basic questions into a couple of paragraphs.

To make your Business Plan credible, you should use and understand the terms and metrics commonly used to describe the performance of rental properties. You will find an explanation of helpful terms such as ADR, Occupancy Rate, RevPAR and more in the Glossary at the end of this book.

The guidance provided in this book will help you to assemble all the information you need to write a good Business Plan but there are two important things to keep in mind: Be realistic! You are enthusiastic about this new business opportunity, but the Business Plan isn't about sharing that enthusiasm; it is a way of demonstrating that this business will be built on good research, sound data and logical financial planning. The other thing to remember is that any Business Plan should be as short as possible. Even Business Plans for large Corporations seldom exceed thirty or forty pages and yours should be much shorter. Give the essential information, but don't get carried away.

2. Before You Start - Planning

Free tool available:

www.theairbnbplaybook.com/tools

THE THREE OPTIONS

Airbnb hosts generally fall into one of three categories;

1. **You already own your own property and you want to list space in it on Airbnb.** This is the simplest option and the most common for Airbnb hosts - you own a property and you intend to rent out part of it on Airbnb.

2. **You rent a property and you want to list it on Airbnb.** This is also fairly common - you already rent a property and you intended to list part of it on Airbnb or you intend to rent a property specifically to list on Airbnb.

3. **You are going to buy a property to list on Airbnb.** This can potentially provide the highest financial returns, but it also involves the highest level of risk. Some people have become successful entrepreneurs through buying property to list on Airbnb and there are now niche mortgage providers who specialize in financing property purchase specifically for Airbnb (though many mainstream mortgage lenders will now also consider this).

In general, Option 1 requires the lowest level of planning and preparation while Option 2 and especially Option 3 require more detailed research and financial planning. You'll find more information on the things that you need to do for each option in the next Chapter.

MARKET AND AREA RESEARCH

From the sections above, it should be clear that effectively researching the accommodation market in the area in which you plan to list a property on Airbnb is absolutely essential to your planning. Having reliable and current data is central to good research and producing a convincing Business Plan. As one prominent person in the industry noted; *'Without data, you're just a person with an opinion.'* You can collect some of this data yourself by analyzing Airbnb listings in your area. The Airbnb search facility makes this fairly simple, but it can be time-consuming, and you may want to create a spreadsheet to record what you find. Fortunately, there are some tools available which make this easier and faster.

AIRDNA

AirDNA is a data service company started in 2014 which provides two main products aimed specifically at Airbnb hosts; *MarketMinder* and *Investment Explorer,* both on a subscription basis. *MarketMinder* is a web app which provides metrics for Airbnb properties. This allows hosts and potential hosts to analyze a particular city or zip/post code area for things like rental demand, seasonality, regulation, and potential for revenue growth. This data is extracted from publically available Airbnb data which is updated daily. *MarketMinder* itself is updated monthly, around the 5th- 8th of each month. *MarketMinder* can also display a map of a selected area showing the location of all Airbnb listed properties and the Average Daily Rate and average Occupancy Rate for all the properties on the map.

MarketMinder also provides the ability to drill-down further to analyze data such as demand for particular sizes of Airbnb property in a selected area, seasonal changes in demand for the selected area and booking lead time for a selected area. AirDNA *MarketMinder* provides quick access to this information, but at a cost.

2. Before You Start - Planning

The AirDNA MarketMinder Dashboard
Image from https://www.airdna.co/

Some basic information is free – just go to the AirDNA site and use the *'Search for a location'* tool. Monthly subscriptions to *MarketMinder* are based on market size and start from $20 per month, though there is generally a one month free trial available if you want to test this product. The higher the level of subscription you select, the more data you will be able to see. A sub-set of the *MarketMinder* data is also available on AirDNA *Rentalizer*, a free rental calculation tool which allows you to enter the address of a property and to see a brief summary of its estimated Airbnb rental potential.

The AirDNA *Investment Explorer* web app is intended for people who want to rent or buy properties to list on Airbnb. It provides detailed rental data to allow you to see how much Airbnb rentals are earning in selected areas as well as tools to compare the average cost to rent or buy versus average Airbnb rental income. *Investment Explorer* is also a subscription service and packages start from $200 per month.

THE AIRBNB PLAYBOOK

The AirDNA Investment Explorer Dashboard
Image from https://www.airdna.co/

MarketMinder is based on a world-wide data set and provides information on every area where there are Airbnb rentals. Both *Investment Explorer* and *Rentalizer* provide data only on Airbnb rentals within the United States.

MASHVISOR

MashVisor is another web-based service, also started in 2014, that allows investors and landlords to assess the potential property. Unlike AirDNA, MashVisor is intended for use by all real estate investors and it does not just provide data from Airbnb listings, it also draws information from other services like Zillow and Redfin.

2. Before You Start - Planning

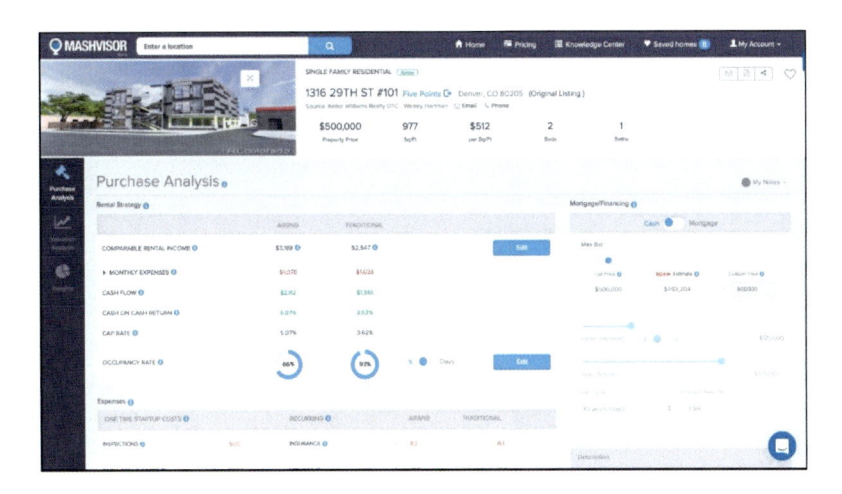

The MashVisor Dashboard
Image from https://www.mashvisor.com

MashVisor combines this information with details of properties for sale from the MLS (Multiple Listing Service – an agglomeration of data from over seventy regional property databases) to present data such as the Airbnb rental potential and the potential Traditional and Airbnb Cash on Cash Return.

Currently, MashVisor only covers property within the United States, though the company intends to expand to other parts of the world in the near future. MashVisor is a subscription service which starts from $25 per month. Two-week free trials are available.

> *Pro-Tip: Understanding the Airbnb market in your area is an essential part of becoming a successful host – whether you do research manually or use the tools described here, take the time to do research before you start.*

TRENDS

Recognizing and reacting to trends in the Airbnb market is as important as finding raw data. Trends can be regional as areas become more or less popular with travelers but they can also be linked to property types as in the recent popularity of *'rustic chic'* – modern properties made to look aged or the popularity of Airbnb properties which emphasize energy efficiency and the use of environmentally friendly appliances and construction and furnishings which use green materials. These trends may be wider still, such as the growth of *'wellness tourism'* in which guests look for rentals close to outdoor activities or amenities such as spas and health centers.

As an Airbnb host, you need to be aware of these trends so that you can react appropriately either by updating your listing, changing your prices or even making changes to your property. Airbnb regularly release reports based on their data which highlight emerging and changing trends. These are an important resource for any existing or potential Airbnb host.

However, Airbnb also provide a trends tool which is available to all hosts and is useful way of planning changes to the rental price of your property. You can find this on the *'Calendar'* screen – it's a small information panel on the right-hand side.

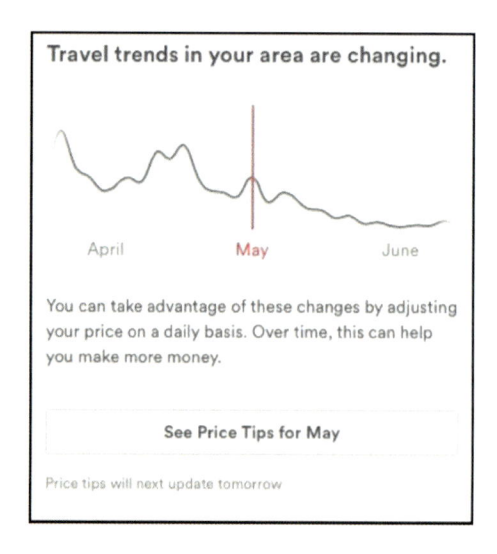

Image from; Airbnb.com

This indicator is based on historical data covering Airbnb rentals as well as information about forthcoming events. Using this tool is a good way of predicting changes in demand in your area which may in turn enable you to change your prices.

2. Before You Start - Planning

TARGET DEMOGRAPHIC

As part of your research, you need to think about the kind of people you are likely to attract as guests. Will you attract mainly business or leisure travelers? Many businesses now use Airbnb as an accommodation provider - is your property in a business district or close to a conference center or other large corporate venue? Alternatively, is your property in the centre of a popular tourist city, near a major tourist destination or in a rural or beachside location?

Will the space you have available for rent likely appeal mainly to individuals, families or large groups? Is your property in an area full of hipster coffee bars and popular music venues or is it located in a quiet, retirement area?

> *Pro-Tip: Identifying your target demographic for guests is of the utmost importance and it will provide essential information for how you decorate and equip your property and how you describe it in your listing. Take the time to think about this right now.*

Think about who your property will appeal to, about nearby attractions and venues and consider your target demographic when writing your listing. Highlight features of your property or location that are likely to appeal to that demographic.

COMPETITION ANALYSIS IN YOUR AREA

As a basic element of your research, you should look at the competition in your area. Use the Airbnb search facility or tools such as AirDNA to find other renters in your area and look at their calendars to see which periods are busy and which are quiet. Do the busy periods correlate to upcoming events? Look at their prices – can you compete with the rental cost of comparable properties and still make money? Can you initially undercut the pricing of competitors to attract guests? Also consider the number of traditional hotels and guesthouses in the area.

COMPETITION IS GOOD!

In some areas, the sheer number of other Airbnb competitors can seem overwhelming. But, if these renters are attracting bookings, that's actually good because it indicates a high level of demand. Conversely, if there is little or no competition in your area, this may indicate a lack of demand. In that sense, the existence of competitors is a good thing.

HOW MUCH MONEY WILL YOUR PROPERTY GENERATE AS AN AIRBNB RENTAL?

SETTING A RENTAL PRICE

Once you have identified the competition in your area and you have looked at rental prices for comparable properties (creating a spreadsheet may help with this), you can consider what your weekday and weekend rental rates can be. You don't want this price to be too high because that may deter potential guests, but you don't want it to be too low either or you will be leaving money on the table, though as a new host, you may want to consider initially undercutting the competition in order to attract bookings and to get a few positive reviews.

Airbnb allows you to set different prices for weekend and weekday rentals. If your target demographic is mainly business travelers, you may want to set your weekday rate as higher and the weekend rate lower. If your main source is leisure guests, you may want to do the opposite.

PRICING TOOLS

When setting a price for your Airbnb rental, you are aiming to hit a level that will maximize your Occupancy Rate while exceeding your expenses. However, what you can reasonably charge may change according to seasonal demand, major events or other factors. So, your ideal Airbnb price for any particular night is not something that is going to be fixed – it should be updated regularly to reflect changes in supply and demand.

Fortunately, there are tools which you can use to automate the dynamic

2. Before You Start - Planning

updating of the price of your Airbnb rental. These include third-party tools such as *PriceLabs* and *Beyond Pricing.* These tools provide a recommended price for your Airbnb rental based not just on data derived from other Airbnb rentals in the area but also by using information such as hotel prices and airline reservations to calculate demand and an appropriate price.

One of the most attractive features of these tools is they can be set to automatically update your Airbnb prices according to changes in demand as well as allowing you to set things like automated last-minute discounts. Both these tools are available as a free demo and if you do decide to adopt either, this will cost 1% of your revenue from Airbnb.

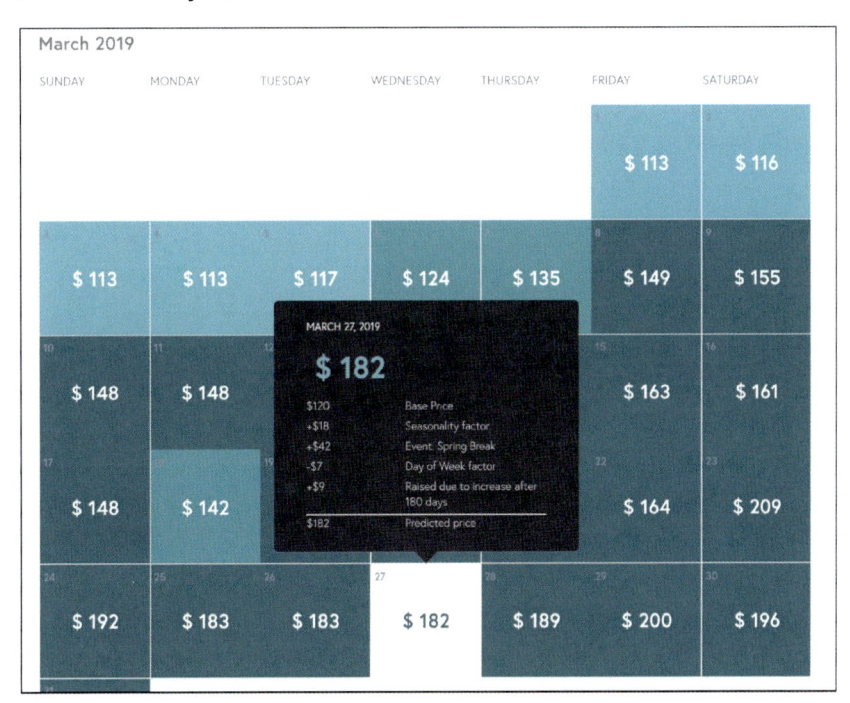

Part of the *Beyond Pricing* dashboard
Image from https://blog.beyondpricing.com/

Do you need automated tools like these to make sure your Airbnb price is always at the optimum level? On a practical level, the answer is no – you can do everything manually using the tools already provided within Airbnb (these are described below). What these tools do is to save you time by automating

THE AIRBNB PLAYBOOK

the process of maintain the optimum price for your property. Can you afford to take the time to do these things yourself? If not, using an automated tool may be worth the expenditure.

If you don't want to invest in a third-party tool, there are features within Airbnb that will help you to ensure that your rental price is always in the right range. Information from the *Airbnb Calculator* is displayed on your calendar. Nights which you have set as available show the price you have set displayed in either green or orange. Prices highlighted in green are likely to be booked and you may want to consider raising the price. Prices highlighted in orange are higher than the average for other properties in the area and you may want to consider reducing them.

Clicking on the highlighted price for any available night will bring up the following information box.

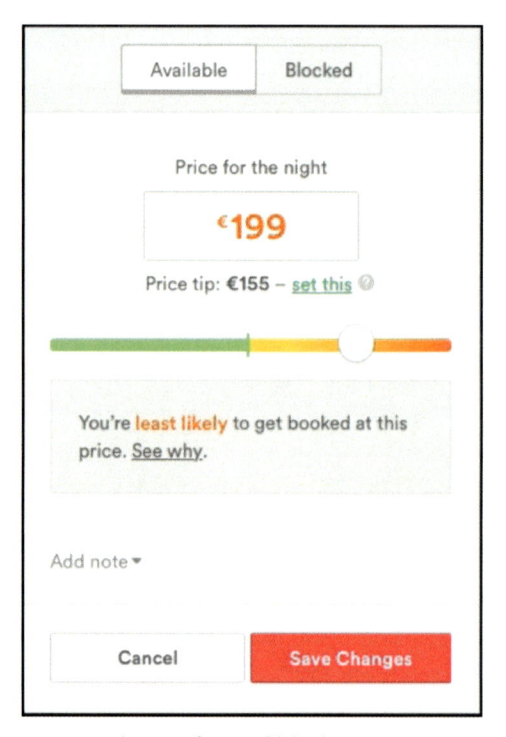

Image from; Airbnb.com

This information box allows you to see how much you will have to reduce

2. Before You Start - Planning

your price to get it into the green zone and provides a *Price Tip* – the price recommended for your property by Airbnb. This is helpful, but according to many users the pricing recommendations are set rather low so it may not be necessary to reduce your price to that recommended by Airbnb to secure bookings. You should also note that the guidance provided in these Airbnb tools is derived solely from other Airbnb bookings in the area and, unlike tools such as *PriceLabs* and *Beyond Pricing,* does not take account of any other data.

You can also see Airbnb recommendations for pricing by clicking on the *'See price tips for…'* button on the *Travel Trends* information panel described earlier. This will show recommended changes for all your prices and with one click you can re-set these to match the Airbnb recommendations. The *Travel Trends* information panel is updated daily and there is currently no way to automate dynamic pricing within Airbnb. You may want to check back every day to see if suggested prices have changed.

> *Pro-Tip: If you want to maximize the potential of your Airbnb listing, the nightly rate is not something you can set once and then forget. It will change seasonally, in time with events and attractions in the area and wider fluctuations in the market. Whether you use an automated system or update it yourself, make sure your rate is always at the optimum level.*

OCCUPANCY RATE

When you are looking at the prices charged by the competition, you will also want to examine their Occupancy Rate – the number of available nights which have actually been booked. Are comparable properties in the area fully booked, or mainly booked only during the weekend or during the week? This will help to estimate your own potential Occupancy Rate which, combined with your planned rental charges, allows you to estimate the potential income you can expect from being an Airbnb host.

If you use tools such as *Beyond Pricing*, *PriceLabs* or *AirDNA*, you will be able to see historic Occupancy Rate data for your property.

EXPENSES

Balanced against income, you also need to think about the costs of becoming an Airbnb host. Here are the main things you need to consider when you are starting out;

- You are likely to need, at the very least, new bedding and towels if not also new appliances, furniture and decoration. How much will this cost? *You can find more information about this in Chapter 4; Equipping, Furnishing and decorating your property.*

- Are you going to do the meeting with guests, handing over keys, checkout and all the cleaning and laundry associated with being an Airbnb host yourself? If so, that will take time and generate costs and you must allow for this.

- Are you going to subcontract any of these tasks to specialist services? If so, you need to allow for these costs in your expenses. *You can find more information about this in Chapter 7; Cleaning and Reset.*

- Are you going to use *AirDNA, Beyond Pricing, PriceLabs* or any of the other specialist tools for Airbnb hosts? How much do these cost each month?

- Will you provide things like toothpaste, soap, shampoo, snacks or beverages for your guests? How much will that cost?

- Will you allow your guests access to your food and beverages? How much will this cost?

- Your utility bills will increase because there are more people in your property, so you also need to factor this in.

- You may need to upgrade your home insurance. How much will this cost? *You can find out more about insurance in Chapter 3; Getting Ready to Start - Preparation*

- You may need an accountant to help you to pay tax on your Airbnb revenue. How much will this cost? *You can find out more about tax for*

2. Before You Start - Planning

Airbnb hosts later in this Chapter.

To help you with controlling your finances there are also subscription-based specialist services and tools available to Airbnb hosts. One of the most popular is *AirGMS* which can be used to automate many Airbnb functions such as messaging, communicating with service providers such as cleaners, completing guest reviews as well as providing a record of your Airbnb income and expenditure.

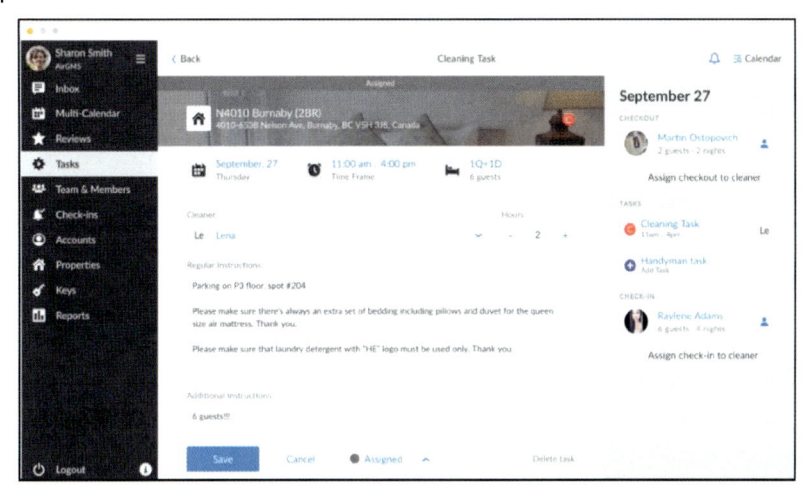

Part of the AirGMS Task Management dashboard
Image from https://www.airgms.com/

You can also download a number of ready-made spreadsheets designed to allow you to track your Airbnb expenses – just *search for 'Airbnb expense tracker'*.

Free tool available:

www.theairbnbplaybook.com/tools

SAFETY AND SECURITY

Safety and security are major concerns for Airbnb hosts and guests. There is a perception that Airbnb is unsafe but, while there have been a small number of serious incidents, Airbnb is actually statistically safer than staying at a hotel. However, as a host this is something you need to consider as part of your planning.

FOR YOU

As an Airbnb host, you are going to be allowing people you have never met to stay in your property. That can be a daunting prospect, but some common-sense planning will help.

ASSESS YOUR GUESTS' PROFILE BEFORE AGREEING TO THE RENTAL

Use Airbnb to read your potential guest's profile and reviews from previous Airbnb hosts. Look for verified phone numbers, connected social networks, and references. If these aren't available, you can ask your guests to provide these. Does the guest have reviews from previous Airbnb hosts – looking at previous reviews is the single most useful way to evaluate potential guests. However, you also have to read between the lines – Airbnb don't like negative reviews of guests (you will find out more about the Airbnb review process in a later chapter). That can mean that hosts are reluctant to post negative reviews, but they won't generally be positive if that isn't true.

A review that says something like; *'Great guest! Pleasure to host these lovely people'* lets you know that the host was truly happy with these guests. If the only comment in the review is *'Arrived on time'*, that may imply that the guest's behavior in other respects wasn't perfect.

Also look at how complete the guest profile is. If you would like more information, consider going back and politely asking the guest to provide more information perhaps asking them to verify their ID with Airbnb before you accept the

2. Before You Start - Planning

booking. Evaluate the messages they send you – do they take the time to write a comprehensible message or do their responses seem rushed?

None of these things on their own should raise a red flag – a guest without reviews may be someone who has only recently joined Airbnb and a person who sends very brief responses may simply be busy. It is important to trust your instincts here – do potential guests respond positively to your messages and/or requests for additional information? Overall, do these seem like people you want to stay in your property?

COMPLETE THE HOUSE RULES AND HOUSE MANUAL IN AIRBNB TO MAKE SURE YOUR GUESTS KNOW WHAT YOU EXPECT

Do you allow smoking? Pets? Children? Do you insist that guests remove their footwear while inside the property? Can they use your food and beverages? Are there areas inside or outside the property where guests aren't permitted? Make your expectations clear from the start so that guests understand what you want.

Free tool available:

www.theairbnbplaybook.com/tools

MAKE SURE YOUR INSURANCE IS APPROPRIATE AND UP TO DATE

Insurance for Airbnb hosts is covered in more detail in the next chapter of this book.

USE SECURITY SYSTEMS IN OFF-LIMIT AREAS

The use of security cameras in Airbnb guest areas is not a good idea because guests may find this intrusive but it is acceptable to use passive security systems like Piper to monitor access to areas you have set as off limits. If you do use a system such as Piper, do inform your guests and explain how it works and what it does in your House Manual.

The Piper Security System
Image from: https://getpiper.com/

BE SENSIBLE!

Don't leave money, jewelry or other valuables or personal information in guest areas.

> **Pro-Tip:** Trust your instincts! If there is something about a guest profile or communication that concerns you, don't hesitate to ask for more information or even to decline the booking.

FOR YOUR GUESTS

Safety and security are also concerns for potential guests and you can take steps to make them feel more secure. Don't forget to note these things in your property listing.

PROVIDE YOUR PROPERTY WITH GOOD SECURITY

This should make guests feel safe but without being intrusive. Security covers not just things like effective locks and alarms for doors and windows but also smoke and carbon monoxide detectors, a fire extinguisher, a first-aid kit, instructions on what to do in the event of a fire and contact information for local authorities and emergency services. Hopefully your guests won't need any of these things, but providing them can help to make them feel both safe and secure.

2. Before You Start - Planning

BE AVAILABLE TO RESPOND TO QUESTIONS OR CONCERNS RAISED BY GUESTS

Make sure that your house manual tells guests how to contact you. You may also want to contact your guests one or two days into their stay to check that everything is OK. Don't do this by turning up at the property unannounced as this can feel like an intrusion on the privacy of your guests – use Airbnb messaging or call them.

IS AIRBNB IS REGULATED IN YOUR AREA?

One thing that any prospective Airbnb host needs to be aware of is that there are a bewildering number of different local regulations. To provide a few examples, in the city of San Francisco Airbnb hosts must be full-time residents, must register with the city authorities and must not rent out for more than ninety nights each year. In Canada, Airbnb hosts must register as businesses. In Barcelona, Airbnb hosts must have a city-approved license and the city authorities regularly check listings and prosecute people who don't have a license. In the city of Santa Monica in southern California, Airbnb hosts must live in the property during the rental period, must apply for a business license before they begin renting and must collect a 14% occupancy tax from guests which is payable to the city authorities.

It is not just regulation specifically aimed at short-term rental that affect Airbnb hosts. Regulations regulating the Real Estate industry may also apply, especially if you are planning on having more than one Airbnb property. In Hawaii, for example, if you manage more than one property, you must be a licensed real estate agent.

Given the number of different regulations which apply not just in different countries but in different cities and that these are constantly being updated, this guide cannot provide full details. As an Airbnb host it is your responsibility to find out what the regulatory requirements in your area are and to ensure that you comply with them.

However, Airbnb do provide some helpful information on this. In the Airbnb help article *'Responsible hosting in the United States'* you will find a listing of many major cities in the US and their regulatory requirements. Similar guidance is provided for some other countries which are important Airbnb locations. Go to the Airbnb help center and in the *'Search'* field type *'responsible hosting in'* followed by the city or area you are interested in to find guidance (if available) for the area in which your property is located.

New York, NY

When deciding whether to become an Airbnb host, it's important for you to understand the laws and Airbnb policies in place in your city. As a platform and marketplace we do not provide legal advice, but we want to provide some useful links that may help you better understand laws and regulations in New York. This list is not exhaustive, but it should give you a good start in understanding your local laws and policies. If you have questions, contact the Department of Buildings, Department of Finance or other city agencies directly, or consult a local lawyer or tax professional.

- **Business Licensing.** You may be required to obtain a special license or permit in New York. For more information, please consult the City's new business portal, the City's business regulation finder, and the New York Administrative Code (available under "ADC" on New York State's website).
- **Multiple Dwelling Law.** The New York State Multiple Dwelling Law restricts renting out a Class A multiple dwelling for periods of fewer than 30 days when the host is not present. The definitions of "Class A" and "multiple dwelling" can be found in Sections 4-7 and 4-8 of Article 1 of the Multiple Dwelling Law. The law exempts rentals to a "boarder, roomer or lodger," which has been interpreted to mean that, in general, if a guest shares the apartment with a permanent resident who is present for the duration of the rental (i.e., a "shared space" rental), it is permissible under the Multiple Dwelling Law.
- **Advertising.** New York State has also banned advertisement for rentals in "Class A" dwellings that are in violation of the Multiple Dwellings Law's restriction on short-term rentals. Penalties on those who are found by the New York City Office of Special Enforcement to be violating this law begin at $1,000 for the first violation.

Part of the Airbnb Guidance on Regulations in New York, NY.
Image: Airbnb

Contact your local authority and ask them whether any of the following apply to Airbnb hosts;

- **Business License.** Do you need a special business license to operate as an Airbnb host in your area?

- **Zoning Rules.** Many areas are covered by zoning codes, planning codes, or city ordinances which govern how properties can be used.

- **Special Permits.** Some areas may require that you have a special permit to operate as an Airbnb host.

- **Taxes.** In addition to paying tax on your income, some areas require guests to pay a special tax for each overnight stay. If this applies to your area, you must collect the required tax and pass it on to the local authority.

2. Before You Start - Planning

- **Building and Housing Standards.** Some areas have special requirements for properties that are rented out and may even require an inspection before you can do this.

REGULATION CAN GIVE YOU A BUSINESS ADVANTAGE!

Probably the single most common mistake that new Airbnb hosts make is to set up without first checking on local regulations. Local authorities are becoming increasingly aware of Airbnb and are carrying out more checks on hosts. People who don't comply with regulations may be fined and even barred from renting out their property. If you comply with regulations while your competitors do not, this can mean that you will stay in business while they are shut down. That is potentially a massive commercial advantage for you!

In your business plan, highlight the regulatory requirements in your area and explain how you will comply with them.

STRATA AND HOUSING ASSOCIATIONS

Strata is an innovation in real estate law that originated in Australia and has been copied around the world. Strata title is often used in apartment blocks and means that the owner has sole title to an apartment and shared title of common areas such as stairs, corridors, gardens and parking areas. Some Strata titles specifically forbid short term rentals of property. In some parts of the world, Housing Associations provide a similar mix of sole and shared title.

Strata buildings and properties operated by Housing Associations have their own rules. These are not laws, but if you contravene these rules you may find yourself subject to legal action. To avoid problems, make sure you check any applicable Strata or Housing Association rules before you start your Airbnb business.

BUSINESS TYPE AND TAXES

Your Airbnb rental is a business and you will be required to pay tax on the money you make. You can approach this in two ways; either you can run a business in your own name or you can create a Limited Liability Corporation (LLC) or another entity. Both have advantages and disadvantages and you should decide which is right for you.

TRADING IN YOUR OWN NAME

You may operate your Airbnb business in your own name, often called a Sole Proprietorship. This means that you report your Airbnb income through your personal income tax assessment. It costs nothing in most places to operate as a Sole Proprietorship and all that is required is that you report your Airbnb as part of your regular tax assessment. Many Airbnb hosts choose this route because it is the simplest and cheapest way of operating. However, a sole proprietor is personally liable for any debts incurred by the business. This means that creditors can seize your home, car or other property to satisfy debts.

TRADING THROUGH AN LLC OR OTHER ENTITY

Alternatively, you can create an LLC for your Airbnb business. Creating an LLC costs money and the tax reporting requirements are generally more complex than for a Sole Proprietorship. However, a key benefit of an LLC is that your liability is limited to the amount of your investment in the LLC.

RISKS

The principal difference between the two options is liability. If you operate your Airbnb business as a Sole Proprietorship, you become legally personally responsible for all debts. If, in a worst-case scenario, you are sued by a guest who is injured or even dies while staying at your property, you may become personally responsible which means that you could potentially lose everything. Operating as an LLC reduces this liability, though it does not remove it entirely.

2. Before You Start - Planning

It is possible to at least partly offset the risks associated with operating as a Sole Proprietorship by ensuring that you have appropriate insurance. However, be aware that if any problems arise through your negligence (if you have faulty appliances in your rental property, for example, or smoke detectors which are not working) your insurance may not cover you and you may still be personally liable.

TAX CONSIDERATIONS

Operating as an LLC can provide tax advantages such as paying a lower rate, but these are often linked to operating as a corporate entity which is more complex. Whether this is a good idea or not depends on how much income you plan to generate through Airbnb. If you are expecting only to make a little extra money now and again, the costs of starting and operating an LLC may outweigh the potential tax advantages. If you intend your Airbnb business to provide a regular secondary income stream or even to provide your main source of income, forming an LLC may be the best and most cost-effective approach.

This is a complex issue and when you are planning to start your Airbnb business, it is a very good idea to get professional help to decide which approach is best for you. Before you do this, you will need to have completed your basic planning and produced a Business Plan so that you can explain what you intend to do and how much money you expect to make. You may then want to talk to an attorney or an accountant about your plans in order to get advice on the best route for you. This will cost, but it will help to give you a sound basis for setting up your Airbnb Business.

CHAPTER 2 KEY POINTS

- ✓ Set goals for your Airbnb business, decide what you want to achieve.

- ✓ Conduct market and area research on the Airbnb market in your area before you start.

- ✓ Check what the competition is doing.

- ✓ Identify the most profitable demographic for your area and set your listing up to attract these guests.

- ✓ Assess whether you have the time and people skills to become a successful Airbnb host or if you should delegate these areas.

- ✓ Calculate how much you can charge for your Airbnb rental and how much it will cost to run. Maximize your nightly rates.

- ✓ Ensure you understand Airbnb regulation in your area and any requirements for reporting.

- ✓ Pick a business vehicle that will suit your needs and minimize your risk.

- ✓ Create a Business Plan that summarizes all of the above and refer back to it on a regular basis.

3

GETTING READY TO START:
PREPARATION

3. Getting Ready to Start - Preparation

Now that the planning is done, it's almost time to actually begin your Airbnb business, but there are a few last things to consider first.

YOU OWN A PROPERTY YOU WANT TO LIST ON AIRBNB

If you own the property you will be using for Airbnb, in addition to ensuring you comply with local regulations, all you need to do is;

CHECK WITH YOUR MORTGAGE LENDER

Some mortgage lenders allow you to rent out parts of your property, some do not. Contact your lender and tell them what you are planning. If your current mortgage does not allow you to rent out part of your property short-term, you may want to switch to a mortgage or lender which does allow this.

If you plan to rent out the whole property, you must tell your lender. Most personal mortgages are on the basis that the property will be your main residence. If instead you plan to rent it out, you may need to switch to a new mortgage.

CHECK WITH THE STRATA/HOUSING ASSOCIATION

The rules of some properties operated under Strata or by Housing Associations may specifically limit or even forbid short-term rentals. If this applies to you, approach the Management Board and ask for permission to rent on Airbnb. Many Boards are not familiar with Airbnb and if you are able to assure them that there won't be inconvenience to neighbors, noise or damage, they may be willing to reconsider.

Some hosts have found that offering to pay part of their Airbnb rental fees into the property management fund (and increasing their rental charges to cover this) helps to persuade the Board to accept this change. It may also be helpful if you can demonstrate that your insurance will cover wear and tear or damage to common areas.

YOU RENT A PROPERTY YOU WANT TO LIST ON AIRBNB

If you already rent a property and you want to rent out part of it on Airbnb, in addition to ensuring you comply with local regulations, all you need to do is;

CHECK WITH YOUR LANDLORD

Your lease may specifically prohibit sub-letting. Don't be tempted to run a rented property as an Airbnb rental without telling your landlord or you may find yourself evicted. You need to persuade the landlord to revoke the *'no sub-letting'* clause from the lease. To achieve this you will need to reassure your landlord that the arrival and departure of guests will not inconvenience other tenants nor cause damage to common areas or to your property and you may need to offer to pay for any legal costs involved in having a new lease drawn-up.

A conscientious landlord may point out that they will need to purchase more expensive short-term rental insurance if they allow you to sub-let on Airbnb. Many Airbnb hosts have found that the simplest solution is to offer the landlord a percentage of the rental income in addition to the rent you pay. It is up to you to decide what percentage you could afford to offer while remaining profitable, but this may be the best, and perhaps only, way to convince a reluctant landlord to allow you to list a rental property on Airbnb. If you come to this sort of agreement with a landlord, do set it down in writing.

RENTING A PROPERTY TO LIST ON AIRBNB

RENTAL ARBITRAGE

If you plan to rent a property specifically to rent through Airbnb you will be doing something called rental arbitrage. This simply means that you will rent out a property at a rate that is less than your costs.

To calculate whether a property has the potential for Airbnb rental arbitrage, it is first necessary to find out the **weighted daily average rate** for comparable Airbnb properties in the area. This is as simple as noting the weekday and

3. Getting Ready to Start - Preparation

weekend rates for other, similar, Airbnb properties in the relevant area. You can find this by looking though Airbnb rentals in the area or by using a tool such as MashVisor or AirDNA. Then, you multiply the average weekday rate by five, the average weekend rate by two, add the two figures together and then divide by seven – the result is the weighted daily average rate for comparable Airbnb properties in your area.

Next, you assess your monthly property expenses including rent/mortgage and other relevant costs. Divide the monthly total by thirty and you have your **daily property expenses** cost.

Finally, divide the **weighted daily average rate** by your **daily property expenses** to arrive at a **rental ratio.** If this is less than 1, you will not be able to cover your property expenses by renting on Airbnb. If the result is exactly 1, then you can cover your property costs by renting on Airbnb, but only if you rent your property out continuously. If you want to make a profit from your property, it is best to aim for a rental ratio of 2 or more as you may not have guests every night.

Assessing the Occupancy Rate of other comparable Airbnb properties in the area will help you to assess the Occupancy Rate you can expect. Using the rental ratio derived through the calculations above and the expected Occupancy Rate, you can assess whether the property you are planning to rent has the capacity for Airbnb rental arbitrage.

RISKS TO CONSIDER IN AIRBNB RENTAL ARBITRAGE

There are several potential risks involved and you must consider these.

- **Changing Market Conditions.** The real estate conditions in any area can change continuously. These can be affected by changes in the overall housing market or other factors in the local area. These can be positive, such as the creation of a new tourist attraction or negative, such as the closure of a large local source of employment. These can affect your ability to attract Airbnb guests.

- **Changing Regulations and Rules.** Airbnb is still relatively new and local regulation and the rules of Strata properties and those controlled by Housing Associations are still changing in accordance. A change in regulation or rules which affects your property may impact your ability to make a profit though Airbnb.

- **Unexpected events.** What happens if your property is in an area that suddenly becomes less attractive because it is affected by a natural disaster or featured in a negative news story? What happens if you become ill? You can't be certain whether any of these things will happen, but you can plan for them. Consider whether you can afford to keep paying the rent if Airbnb rentals decrease or stop for a few months. Can you quit your rental agreement if for any reason Airbnb rentals drop off? What period of notice do you have to give?

When you are planning to rent a property to rent through Airbnb, you need to consider the unexpected and to ensure your plans include sufficient leeway to allow you to deal with these potential issues.

CONVINCING THE LANDLORD

If you are renting a property with the intention of renting it on Airbnb, you must make sure that the terms of your lease do not forbid or limit sub-letting. You may need to persuade the landlord to agree to the removal of such a clause. You can explain that this will assure a regular payment of the rent, and the fact that the property may not be occupied every night means a reduction in wear and tear.

You will also need to provide assurances that the arrival and departure of guests will not inconvenience other tenants. In many cases, the best way to persuade a landlord to rent out a property which will be used as an Airbnb rental is to offer to share a percentage of the rental fees. If you do this, you will need to allow for this when setting your rental price and to get the agreement confirmed in writing.

RENTAL ARBITRAGE REGULATION

One thing that you will need to check is whether there are any laws or regulations which govern rental arbitrage in your area. In most areas, the only requirement is that you report your earnings for tax purposes but you need to be certain there are no additional requirements in your area and if there are, consider how you will comply.

BUYING A PROPERTY TO LIST ON AIRBNB

If you are considering buying a property specifically to rent out on Airbnb, you don't have to worry about persuading the landlord, but you will face other issues.

FINDING FINANCE

Although the buy-to-let market has existed for some time, until recently many lenders were reluctant to provide finance for properties which were to be rented out through Airbnb. Lenders felt that, although Airbnb short-term letting has the potential to deliver higher returns that traditional, long-term rental, this was a risky investment strategy. However now that Airbnb is well established and recognized as the industry leader and an important element of the accommodation industry in some areas, things are changing.

Many mortgage lenders now see Airbnb as a legitimate way of producing a reasonable return from a property asset. Many are now less wary of Airbnb properties and many mainstream providers will now consider mortgages for this purpose.

However, an investment mortgage can differ from a mortgage for the purchase of a primary residence in many ways. The most notable is the interest rate – on a mortgage for an investment property, the interest is typically 0.5% – 1.5% higher than for a primary residence mortgage. The reason for this is that lenders assess investment mortgages as being higher risk and to compensate, they look for a higher return.

Investment mortgages typically also involve a higher percentage of the total price paid by the buyer as a deposit (up to 25%) and more complex application paperwork. You will also have to demonstrate that you have researched the financial implications of buying to let – your Business Plan will provide most of what is required, and some lenders will want to see evidence that you have successfully managed rented property before.

What if you already own a home, but you want to move out and rent it on Airbnb? Some lenders will consider this, though generally only if you can satisfy them that you originally bought the property as a residence and your decision to move out and use it as a rental property came later and for unforeseen circumstances. If you are in this situation, you must apply to your lender for *'consent to let'* but be aware that if they agree, they may charge a higher interest rate and require an arrangement fee.

Don't be tempted to apply for a mortgage for a property you want to rent out on Airbnb without informing the lender. Most lenders will allow you to rent out a part of your property, or even the whole of your property for short periods in certain circumstances but if a primary residence mortgage is used to buy a property which is to be rented out full-time, you are committing fraud and you could find yourself in a great deal of trouble.

FIND THE CORRECT LENDER

One way of simplifying the task of finding a lender who is prepared to finance a property purchased for rental on Airbnb is to use a mortgage broker. A mortgage broker does not provide finance directly, instead they act as an intermediary, dealing with a number of potential lenders. There are advantages and disadvantages to using a mortgage broker.

A mortgage broker will have access to a wider range of potential sources of finance than a bank and these may include major banks, small lenders and private trusts. Mortgage brokers may also have access to better rates and they are familiar with a range of mortgage types – an important consideration if you are seeking something a little different such as a mortgage for an Airbnb property.

3. Getting Ready to Start - Preparation

If you approach a bank directly, you will have access to a narrower range of products, because the bank will only want to sell you one of their mortgages, and they may have less knowledge of specialist investment mortgages. Set against that, if you already have a relationship with a bank and this may streamline the process for approving the loan. A bank may also be able to provide information and guidance on other financial products such as insurance.

Finding a lender for a mortgage on a property to be used for Airbnb rentals is no different to finding a mortgage for any other investment property. You need to put time and effort into finding a lender who will consider your proposal (or use a mortgage broker to do this for you) and you need to understand what information the lender will need to see in support of your application. You need to be able to provide a viable Business Plan underpinned by credible data and it may be helpful if you can demonstrate previous experience of successfully managing an Airbnb rental property.

For those in the US seeking to re-finance a property used for Airbnb rentals, Airbnb has an initiative with four major lenders, Fannie Mae, Quicken Loans, Citizens Bank and Better Mortgage to allow the submission of Airbnb Proof of Income in support of a refinance loan application.

Pro-Tip: Whether you are renting or buying, make sure that your landlord/lender knows what you are doing and are happy with your Airbnb rental plans. Don't be tempted to go ahead without telling them – this will only cause problems later on.

PUTTING IT ALL TOGETHER
INSURANCE

Many beginner Airbnb hosts assume that they don't need insurance – after all, you already have home insurance, the Airbnb *Host Guarantee* and the free Airbnb *Host Protection Insurance* which covers every host. However, this is incorrect and as an Airbnb host, you need to carefully consider your insurance situation.

In the small print of most home insurance policies you will find a *'business pursuit's exclusion'*. This means that the insurance company can deny any claim associated with carrying out a business in the property. Airbnb rentals are a business and so any claim for damage caused by guests during a stay may be excluded. It is very important that you talk to your home insurance provider before you begin Airbnb rentals and ensure that you are covered. This may entail a new policy and higher premiums, something you need to allow for when you calculate your expenses.

The Airbnb *Host Guarantee* covers damage to your property caused by and Airbnb guest, but it does have limitations – for example, it does not cover the theft of cash or high-value items. Airbnb note that the Host Guarantee *'should not be considered a replacement or stand-in for homeowners or renters insurance.'*

The Airbnb *Host Protection Insurance* automatically covers every Airbnb booking, and it covers hosts against third-party claims of injury or property damage related to an Airbnb stay up to a maximum of one million dollars. However, this too has limitations - despite its name it is not an underwritten insurance policy and it does not apply to every country in which there are Airbnb rentals.

It is clearly sensible to have liability insurance and in areas where a permit or license is required to operate an Airbnb rental evidence of liability insurance may be compulsory. The Airbnb *Host Protection Insurance* scheme will generally not be accepted and renters must provide their own liability insurance. Many lenders also require an investment property to be adequately insured for the purpose for which it is to be used. If you are buying a property to use as an Airbnb rental, you will need appropriate damage and liability insurance.

Fortunately, as Airbnb becomes more and more popular, insurance providers are recognizing the need to provide appropriate policies. Research suggests that failure to have adequate insurance is a problem for a large percentage of Airbnb hosts. Make sure you don't fall into this category.

3. Getting Ready to Start - Preparation

AIRBNB SECURITY DEPOSIT

When you set the price for your Airbnb listing, you also have the option to add a security deposit in the *Extra Charges* section to cover any damage to your property. This can be set at anything between $100 and $5,000 but it may not work in the way that you expect. The guest does not actually have to pay this deposit before they stay – instead, by making a booking in a rental that includes a security deposit, they are agreeing that they will be liable for up to the amount of the deposit if there are damages. If a host makes a claim through the Airbnb Resolution Center within 14 days of a guest stay, some of that agreed deposit may be requested from the guest to cover damages.

> *Pro Tip: It's important to understand that the Airbnb Host Guarantee and Host Protection Insurance are not substitutes for having appropriate home and liability insurance.*

MAINTAINING YOUR PROPERTY

Maintenance is an issue for any homeowner or renter, but it becomes even more significant when you are an Airbnb host. Clearly, your property needs to be structurally sound, in good order, secure, bug-free and compliant with any local fire and building regulations. To keep your guests happy and your reviews positive, you must also keep your property adequately maintained. For the most part, this is common sense;

- Make sure that décor, carpets, furniture and beds in guest areas are clean and in good order,

- Remove potential tripping hazards or clearly mark them,

- Make sure that bedding, towels and linens are clean and fresh,

- Make sure that all appliances and gadgets are working as they should, and all wiring and plumbing is in good order,

- If your property includes common areas or outside spaces, make sure that these are also in good order,

- If you provide pots and pans, crockery, cooking utensils, glasses and cutlery, make sure these are present and in good order,

- If you provide food and/or beverages for your guests, make sure these are available and fresh,

- Keep guest areas as clear of your own items and clutter as possible.

None of these things are difficult, but they all take time and cost money to achieve. Have you budgeted adequately for these in your expenses and estimate of the time required? Of course, you can subcontract things like greeting guests, cleaning, laundry and the maintenance of outside spaces to specialist services. This will save time, but again, you must allow for this in your cost estimates.

If you are doing your own cleaning and preparation, creating a checklist of things you need to check and/or clean may be a good idea. That way, you're less likely to forget to check things like whether the microwave needs cleaning or to fail to notice that a glass or cup has been broken.

Have contingency plans in place. If an appliance suddenly fails or your guests need the services of a plumber or electrician, be ready to respond quickly. Guests will become unhappy and may leave a negative review if something described in your listing isn't available or doesn't work correctly.

CHAPTER 3 KEY POINTS

✓ Check with your Landlord, Strata or Mortgage lender before listing your property on Airbnb.

✓ Rental arbitrage can work very well in certain areas, were the average nightly rate is at least 2x the average daily expenses of the property.

✓ Find a lender willing to provide a mortgage for an Airbnb investment property by looking at non-traditional providers.

✓ Get adequate liability insurance as a minimum.

✓ Make sure your property is always in immaculate condition and well maintained.

4
PREPARING
YOUR PROPERTY

4. Preparing your property

MUST-HAVE FEATURES

There are some essential things you must provide in your Airbnb rental. Some of these are fairly obvious – most guests will expect as a minimum access to the Internet, comfortable beds, comfortable seating that can accommodate all the people likely to be staying and space for their belongings. You can assess other important features by looking at your competitors, other Airbnb rentals in the area. All Airbnb listings include a detailed list of amenities. Take some time to look through your competitors' listings and see what they are offering. Can you match or exceed these?

Looking at the listings of your Airbnb competitors is a good way of assessing what the *'must-have'* features in your property will be. If you are going to charge equivalent rates and attract guests, you are going to match or exceed the things that they offer.

FURNISHING, DECORATING AND EQUIPPING YOUR AIRBNB RENTAL PROPERTY

COLOR AND THEMES

In general, keep colors neutral. Bright colors can work for some people but put others off. Keeping colors neutral means that you can appeal to the greatest number of potential guests. Browns and grays for things like carpets and large items of furniture such as sofas are also good because they are easier to keep clean and less prone to showing wear and tear. Look at the photographs of your Airbnb competitors, especially those that have a good occupancy rate. Can you use any of their ideas?

Image: Airbnb Media Resources

When considering decoration and colors, can you find a theme for your property? Is it a beachside home? Add beach-themed accessories to give it a beach-bungalow feel. Do you have a property in a rural area? Add furniture and accessories that give it a rustic, log-cabin feel. Do you have a modern, city-center apartment? Keep it simple and light with modern furniture and appliances. Is your main target demographic business travelers? Provide good workspace including space for computers and printers. Is your main target demographic families? Consider play areas and providing toys and games for children.

Think about who you are planning to target as guests and choose colors and themes that will appeal to them, but don't do anything so extreme that it likely to put others off.

ENTRANCE

First impressions matter and the entrance area of your property is the first thing that guests will see, so make sure it's clean and tidy and provides storage space for coats, shoes, umbrellas and other outdoor items. Keep the space in the entrance and especially between the entrance and guest area as free from clutter as possible – your guests will be arriving with luggage and they want a clear path to where they will be staying. Use a doormat at the entrance and at any access to balconies or other outside areas.

4. Preparing your property

LIVING SPACES

Your guests will want a comfortable place to gather and to watch television or chat. This space must contain at least one comfortable seat for every potential guest. Use inexpensive items such as throw blankets, accent pillows and wall decorations to give this space style and character and to extend your chosen theme.

KITCHENS AND DINING AREAS

Kitchens should be clean and tidy and as clutter-free as possible. Dining areas must have sufficient space to accommodate every potential guest. Dinnerware, utensil holders, condiment holders, food storage jars and table linen can be used to accent your chosen color scheme and theme and to provide a pulled-together look that guests will appreciate.

Kitchens should be provided with dish soap, a scrubber or sponge cleaner, spray surface cleaner and paper kitchen roll. If you have a dishwasher, provide dishwasher solution or tablets. If you don't have a dishwasher, provide a drying rack for washing-up. If your kitchen includes a washer, provide appropriate laundry soap.

As a minimum, your kitchen should be provided with hotplates/burners and an oven, a microwave, an electric kettle and/or a coffee maker, a toaster, a kitchen timer, a fridge, and storage spaces for food. Even if you don't provide food for your guests, do make sure your kitchen is provided with salt, pepper, sugar and olive oil.

In terms of equipment, provide at least one sharp knife and a cutting board, at least one cast-iron or non-stick skillet and at least one large pot. Provide sufficient clean cutlery, plates, bowls, cups, mugs and glasses so that there is at least one of everything for each guest. Don't forget a corkscrew, a bottle and/or tin opener, a wooden spoon and a wooden spatula, scissors, tongs and a whisk.

A good way to check the equipment in your kitchen is to spend some time in your Airbnb property before you receive your first guests. Make breakfast and make and serve at least one meal. This is a good way to check if anything is missing.

BEDROOM

The bedroom is the place where your guests will spend most of their time in your property, and it is the place where you will also want to spend time on decorating and equipping. Make sure that the bed and mattress are comfortable and that the bedding is adequate. To check, spend at least one night in there yourself. Were you cold? Was there anything missing or that prevented you from sleeping well? Did the lack of a bedside lamp stop you from reading in bed? If so, fix these problems before your guests arrive!

Image: Airbnb Media Resources

Choose bedding sets that accent your chosen color scheme and theme and add items such as extra pillows and throws to add visual interest. Have extra bedding available in case the weather changes. Ensure that all bedrooms have enough storage and hanging space for guest's clothes and belongings.

4. Preparing your property

BATHROOM

Provide towels and shower curtains in colors that match your style and theme. Provide one set of towels for each guest. Provide bathmats and non-slip mats for showers. Include extra toilet paper, tissues, a cleaning wand for the toilet and a plunger. Provide shower or bath soap, shampoo and conditioner and hand-washing gel or soap.

FINISHING TOUCHES

Finishing touches are the little, extra things that you can do to make your guests' stay more memorable and better. Here are some examples of finishing touches that other Airbnb hosts have included – can you use any of these in your property?

- Create a welcome basket with the makings of a warm drink, cookies and chocolate.

- Provide a basket of snacks.

- Leave a chocolate on the pillow of each guest.

- Add a few spa products to your bathroom.

- Provide a good selection of books, magazines, and listing publications which relate to the local area.

- Put a vase of fresh-cut flowers in the living space.

- Leave a one-size-fits-all bathrobe in the closet, one for each guest.

- Provide spare light bulbs and trash bags.

- Put your telephone number (or email) on the key ring you give guests with the keys for the property and include a clip to attach the keys to a belt or backpack.

Image: Airbnb Media Resources

ITEMS GUESTS USUALLY FORGET

There are certain things that every Airbnb rental should have which don't count as basic amenities, but which your guests may forget to bring with them. Providing these will make your guests happy and improve your ratings.

- Umbrellas, raincoats, and rain boots.

- Sunscreen.

- A hairdryer – Airbnb co-founder Nathan Blecharczyk has claimed that providing guests with a hairdryer is worth an extra $10 per night!

- An iron and ironing board.

- A universal adaptor for electrical appliances.

- A USB and/or iPhone charger.

- Re-usable water bottles.

- A digital clock with an alarm.

- Ear plugs, nail clippers, brush, comb, deodorant.

4. Preparing your property

APPLIANCES

There are no rules about what an Airbnb rental must provide, but there are certain things that guests are going to expect. Look at your competitors' listings – can you match or exceed what they offer? Consider the following;

- An HD television,
- A washing machine,
- A Wi-Fi router (don't forget to tell your guests the password!),
- Heaters and/or fans,
- A vacuum cleaner,

We have already covered what appliances you need in a kitchen but, even if your property does not include a kitchen that guests can use, consider providing a mini-fridge and an electric kettle in guest areas.

When you are buying appliances for an Airbnb rental property, do remember that these will get more wear and tear in a short-term rental property than in the average home. Sometimes, paying a little more for a good quality item is worthwhile and remember, anything you buy to equip an Airbnb rental is a business expense which can be deducted from profits to reduce your tax bill.

> *Pro-Tip: Spend at least a few nights in your Airbnb rental (or have family or friends stay over) using only the facilities, equipment and appliances you provide for guests. In this way, you will quickly notice anything that's missing, or which could be improved.*

MUST-HAVE GADGETS

Some gadgets will improve your guests' experience as well as helping you. Look at what your competitors are offering, but here are some suggestions to begin;

- Smart locks. There are many different forms of keyless entry systems, some even use apps downloaded to a phone (though most can also use keys if your guests don't have a phone). Guests like these and they mean you don't have to meet with your guests to retrieve keys when they check-out.

- A safe or lockbox where guests can leave small items.

- Digital guides. As an alternative to printed copies of local guides, consider going digital. You can provide links to an existing guide that guests can use on their phone or you can use a service like Yourwelcome a rental property welcome app on a touch-screen tablet which can connect guests with local attractions.

Image: https://www.yourwelcome.com/

- In-home entertainment. Consider things like Chromecast, a dongle which plugs into the HDMI port on your television to turn it into a smart TV with access to things like Netflix, YouTube and Spotify. Also provide an HDMI cable to that guest can connect their smart phones or laptops to the TV.

- Wireless thermostat. Systems like Nest by Google allow you to purchase thermostats that can be controlled from your smart phone. Some include motion sensors to automatically activate heating or air conditioning when guests arrive.

4. Preparing your property

- Bluetooth speaker. This will allow your guests to play their music or listen to the radio on their smart phone or laptop.

Free tool available:

www.theairbnbplaybook.com/tools

INFORMATION, GUIDEBOOKS AND LOCAL TRAVEL GUIDES

All Airbnb hosts should provide a hard copy of their house manual. This is something you will create when you write your Airbnb listing and it covers things like house rules but also descriptions of things like how to use the facilities and appliances in the property, the Wi-Fi password, how to use things like keyless entry systems, what the requirements for recycling are, where safety items such as the fire extinguisher and first aid kit are kept and where to park. All guests will be able to see this when they book, but also provide a hard copy in case they aren't able to access when they are staying.

The house manual should also provide instructions on what to do in the event of a fire (including which exits to use) and contact information for local authorities and emergency services as well as a telephone number/email where you can be reached if there is a problem.

All guests will also appreciate information about the local area. Provide a good, local map and multiple copies of any brochures or guides to the area, amenities and attractions. Include information about travel and public transportation as well as parking. If you have great local restaurants, takeaways, or bars, include descriptions, menus and contact details. Personal recommendations and experiences should be included where possible.

Airbnb also provide a travel and leisure information service called *Neighborhoods*. This covers around twenty major Airbnb locations around the world and gives extensive information for travelers. If your property is in one of these areas, include a link in your listing.

Part of the Airbnb Neighborhoods listing for London

GUEST BOOK

You may wish to provide a guest book where your Airbnb guests can write comments about their stay. This can be a great resource for you as a host – it can help to tell you what you are doing right and what you have missed. If a guest comments on something that you had forgotten and that you then include, you can add your own comment thanking them for their suggestion and noting how you have fixed the problem.

SUGGESTION BOX

In addition, you may also wish to include a suggestion box, a place where guests can provide suggestions about improving the experience of staying at your property. Just like the Guest Book, this is a good way to learn how to improve your property and your guests' experience.

PETS

Before you start renting, you need to decide whether you are going to allow guests to bring pets to your property? Allowing pets can give you a larger potential pool of guests – some estimates suggest that less than 10% of Airbnb rentals allow pets so this can dramatically reduce your potential competition. However, pets mean extra work for you and additional things to think about. Dogs can chew, some may have fleas or other parasites which they may leave

4. Preparing your property

behind, and all dogs will leave hair on carpets and furniture. A wet dog can leave a lingering smell that can be difficult to remove. These may mean extra and more intensive cleaning for you and that means extra time and cost.

If you rent an apartment, will your neighbors be happy to meet a dog in common areas? Can you charge an additional fee for a pet to compensate? Some Airbnb hosts count dogs as guests and request an additional payment for each dog while other request an additional fee for pets, payable when guests check-in.

If you do decide to allow pets, don't forget to add contact details for a local veterinarian in your House Manual and make it clear if there are areas in which pets are not allowed. Also consider providing feeding bowls and a pet bed area in your property.

If you have pets and you are renting space in a property, do be considerate of guests. Not everyone wants to be jumped on by a lively dog or joined in bed by a friendly cat. If you do have pets in your home, make this clear in your listing, even though you intend to keep them away from guests. Some people are allergic to animal hair and they will not want to stay in a property where this may be present. Other people may not appreciate being introduced to your pet python or tarantula.

CHAPTER 4 KEY POINTS

- ✓ Use a theme when decorating and furnishing your property.

- ✓ Think about what appliances, gadgets and equipment are essentials and what you can add to make your listing standout. The automatic guest check in system YourWelcom.com is an excellent option.

- ✓ Think about small finishing touches that will enhance your guests experience and make them feel special.

- ✓ Assemble a guest information pack using resources such as Neighberhoods.com

- ✓ Consider providing a Guest Book and a Suggestion Box as they are great tools for getting feedback and improving.

- ✓ Decide whether you are going to accept pets and have a pet policy for your listing.

5
LISTING
YOUR PROPERTY

5. Listing your property

Your Airbnb listing is the main way that you will appeal to potential guests. A good listing may be the difference between creating a viable Airbnb business and failing. Take the time to understand what you want your listing to achieve and create something that highlights the best features of your property and is focused on your target demographic.

Free tool available:

www.theairbnbplaybook.com/tools

OVERVIEW OF THE AIRBNB LISTING PROCESS

HOST PROFILE

When creating your Airbnb listing, you will see a section titled *'Describe Yourself'*. This is where you introduce yourself as an Airbnb host and it's separate from the property listing. This is a good chance to introduce yourself, to talk about your interests and travel experiences and to explain what you hope to achieve as an Airbnb host in terms of providing a positive guest experience. Keep it short, guests don't want to read your autobiography, but tell people enough about you to understand who you are in a few sentences. Include a photograph and describe your main language and any other languages you are familiar with (or have difficulty with). Be honest and open but don't include personally identifying information or anything that might break Airbnb rules by being sexist, racist or offensive in any other way.

TITLE

The title of your Airbnb listing is more important than you might think. It's one of the first things that a potential guest will see and you need to think about how to make it stand out from all the other titles they will be looking at.

Image: Airbnb

This is what potential guests see in search results.

First of all, your Airbnb listing title can have up to just 50 characters (not including spaces), so you don't have much space to play with. You can use symbols such as '&' and common abbreviations such as 'A/C' and *'apt'*, but don't abbreviate to the point where your title is incomprehensible.

The best titles use a single adjective to highlight your property's features, followed by a brief description of the facilities and a note of nearby attractions or venues. You don't need to specify the location in the title – that will already be evident to people using the Airbnb search facility. Don't use generic adjectives like *'great,' 'awesome,'* or *'cool'*. Use words that highlight the best features of your property. *'Modern', 'rustic,' 'spacious'* and *'luxury',* for example, are all good. Then use as few words as possible to describe the type of property; *'apartment,' 'room,' 'house'* or *'cottage'* are all good. Then note nearby attractions or venues or list the main highlight of your property. Any of the following would make good Airbnb listing titles;

5. Listing your property

- *Modern 1BR apt with A/C 5 mins walk from convention center*
- *Rustic 2BR cottage rural area close to hiking trails*
- *Family friendly 4BR condo close to beach*
- *Luxury 1BR apt city center 5 mins walk from subway*

Focus on the first four or five words in particular – on some mobile devices and tablets, that is all that potential guests will see when they see your listing on screen. Do take the time to think about your listing title and how to make it stand out. Look at your competitors' listing titles – do they have good ideas you can copy or bad things that you want to avoid?

DESCRIPTION

The property description is the heart of your Airbnb listing. This is the place where you can tell people all the great things about your property but be cautious – people just don't want to read lots of text. Keep it short and simple and divide it up into short sections using the Airbnb subheadings. Remember, not all your guests will be looking for the same information. A family may want to know about sleeping arrangements for the children and areas for play, but a group of hikers may be more interested in how close you are to a walking trail. Make it easy for any potential guest to find the information they are looking for.

You want to achieve balance in your description. You want to write something that highlights your property's features and is attractive to potential guests, but you also want to manage expectations by not promising too much. Be honest but make sure you point out all the good things about your property. Think about your target demographic – emphasize the things that will appeal to them.

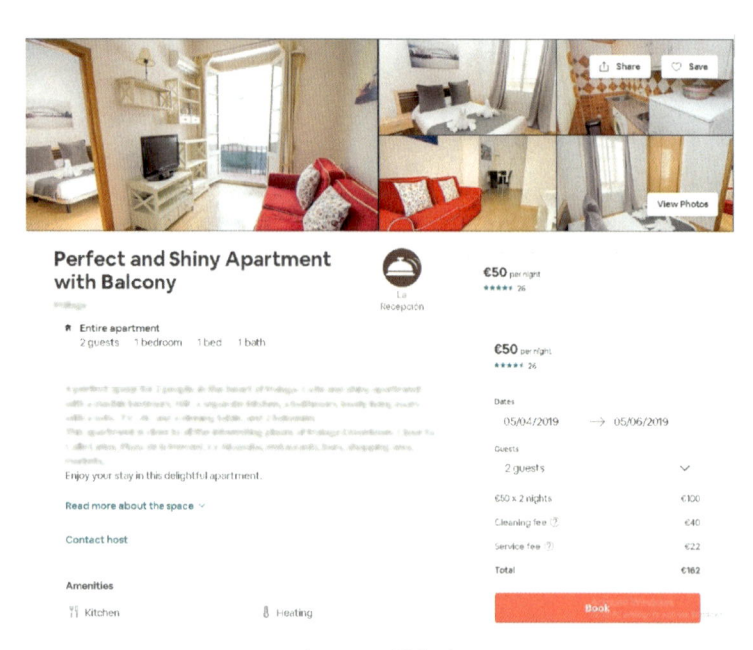

Image: Airbnb

DESCRIPTION TITLE

Just like your listing title, the description title is important and, this time you are limited to 35 characters. Use at least one good adjective and then try to briefly summarize the main appeal of your property. For example;

- ✓ Modern city center apt with parking
- ✓ Luxury rural retreat for romantic breaks

DESCRIPTION SUMMARY

Next, you have a short summary which is limited to 250 words. This is your chance to engage with potential guests so that they want to read more. If they don't like what they see here, they probably won't read any more. Include at least two or three of your property's main selling points and information on its location. Keep thinking about your target audience – what might they be looking for. You may want to include the total size of the space here in square feet or meters.

DETAILED DESCRIPTION

There are several sub-headings here – try to provide information in each. In *The Space*, tell guests about the property. Mention room sizes, styles, age, condition, parking, security and any notable facilities, areas or surroundings. Tell them how many people can sleep there and if there are any temporary beds available if required.

In *Guest Access* explain which parts of the property guests will have access to and which they won't. In *Interaction with Guests*, explain how you can be contacted and whether you will be around while your guests are staying. Explain what happens when they arrive and when they leave.

In *The Neighborhood*, explain what there is in the vicinity of your property. Is it close to lots of great bars, coffee shops and quirky eating places? Tell your guests about them. Is it near the beach or in a beautiful rural location? Tell your guests about the great hiking and the wonderful sunsets. Explain how far your property is from important amenities, venues or attractions – rather than giving a distance, tell them how long it takes to walk or drive to these places.

In *Getting Around* you can tell your guests about how they can travel in the area near your property. Is a car essential to reach your property? Is public transport within walking distance? Are there cycle routes nearby?

The *Other Things to Note* section is where you fill in anything else that didn't fit into any of the other sections. This can also be the place where you want to point out any things about your property that are not so wonderful. Is it an old property with cranky plumbing and low water pressure? This is the place to mention that. Are mosquitoes a problem in the evening? Is parking likely to be an issue? Is traffic noise a problem? Do you have several lively dogs which run around the property? Anything that might affect your guests should go here. It's better to be honest rather than to have unhappy guests leaving bad reviews.

> *Pro-Tip: Your Airbnb listing including photographs is the primary way that you will attract guests. Look at the listings of your competitors, learn from them and take the time to make your listing the best it can be.*

RULES AND RESTRICTIONS

The *House Rules* part of the description is where you provide the contents of your House Manual.

- Do you allow smoking in certain areas inside or outside or not at all?
- Do you allow pets?
- Are their quiet hours?
- May guests bring visitors to your property?
- Can they have parties?
- Do you allow guests to eat and drink only in certain areas?
- Are there off-limit areas for guests?

If there is anything that you want your guests to do or not to do, this is where you should put it. Be clear about your expectations.

Free tool available:

www.theairbnbplaybook.com/tools

CANCELLATION POLICY

Airbnb offer hosts the option to choose one of three cancellation policies. These are *Flexible* (guests can cancel up to 24 hours before they are due to arrive and receive a full refund), *Moderate* (guests can cancel up to five days before they are due to arrive and receive a full refund) and *Strict* (guests only receive a full refund if they cancel less than 48 hours after making the booking and at least 14 days before they are due to arrive).

Decide what is right for you. It may be tempting to go for the *Strict* policy to help assure your cash-flow, but will this deter potential guests? When you receive a request to book from a guest, you will be able to see a history of how many Airbnb bookings this person has cancelled in the previous twelve months.

5. Listing your property

Airbnb also offer other cancellation policies in certain circumstances and policies which apply only to long-term bookings – you can find details of these on the Airbnb site.

Free tool available:

www.theairbnbplaybook.com/tools

PHOTOGRAPHS

The photographs of your property which you upload to your Airbnb listing are one of the first things that any potential guest will look at, so they are very important. You will be able to designate one of your photographs as your cover picture and this photograph, along with the listing title and the price, is what potential guests will first see when they search Airbnb. Because photographs are an important part of your listing, many Airbnb hosts get professional photographers to take the pictures. If you use a professional, make sure you point out the features that you particularly want to emphasize and think about a cover picture – this should be an image that encapsulates the best features of your property.

If you decide to take your own photographs, there are a few things to bear in mind. If you use a phone, don't use the vertical mode because these pictures won't fit well into the Airbnb format. Make sure rooms are clean and tidy and then take at least one photograph of each guest space in good lighting and at least one outside shot of the property, if possible, on a bright, sunny day. Take photographs of any features of the property you want to highlight. Use the captions feature to make sure potential guests know what they are looking at.

Review your photographs and make sure they are clear and sharp. Think about what they show – does the property look gloomy because you took the photographs on a rainy day? Perhaps it's best to try again in better weather. Do rooms look small and cramped? Try again, shooting from the corners of the rooms and use a wide-angle lens if you have one. You cannot edit photographs once they are in Airbnb, so make sure you are happy with them before you upload.

Image: Airbnb Media Resources

This photograph makes this property look light, spacious and inviting.

The minimum picture size for Airbnb is 1024 x 683 pixels. Higher resolution pictures are fine as long as they have an aspect ratio of 3:2 – that's why vertical format pictures from phones don't work well.

CALENDAR

You can set how far in advance guests can book your property. The maximum is one year, and you can charge a premium for booking more than three months in advance. However, if you choose this option, do make sure that you are aware of any upcoming events which may allow you to charge a higher rate.

5. Listing your property

INSTANT BOOK, ONE NIGHT MINIMUM AND ADDITIONAL GUESTS

INSTANT BOOK

One of the options you can set in your Airbnb listing is *Instant Book*. This feature means that potential guests can book instantly for available dates without having to wait for your approval. Selecting this option can generate more interest by moving your listing up the search results – Airbnb promote listings with the best chance to receive a booking, and the convenience of the *Instant Book* feature makes these more likely to achieve bookings.

Hosts who use *Instant Book* may receive more bookings because potential guests can filter search results to show only hosts who offer *Instant Book.* In certain circumstances (for example, if someone is searching for a booking only a few days ahead), this filter may even be automatically applied. Using the *Instant Book* feature can even help you to reach Superhost status because it ensures a good response rate.

The downside to using this feature is that it removes part of your control over vetting potential guests. However, if you do choose *Instant Book* for your listing, you can set several parameters to narrow the range of potential guests to which it applies and limit the terms of their booking. The options are;

- **House Rules.** All guests using *Instant Book* must agree to your house rules.

- **Additional Guest Requirements.** All guests who book through Airbnb must meet Airbnb verification requirements, though these are fairly relaxed. If you choose *Instant Book* for your listing you can set two further guest requirements; You can choose only to allow guests who have received positive reviews from other Airbnb hosts use this feature and you can also limit this feature only to guests who have verified their identity by providing Government-issued ID.

- **Notice and length of stay.** You can also specify the minimum period of notice required for the *Instant Book* feature from same-day bookings to seven days. In addition, you can specify the minimum and maximum length of *Instant Book* stays. If you don't set a maximum, Airbnb will automatically limit *Instant Book* stays to a maximum length of 14 nights.

You can set an automated message to be sent to guests who book using this feature and you can then evaluate their reply to this message. If you are 'uncomfortable' (this is the rather ambiguous term used by Airbnb) with the booking for any reason, you can cancel without penalty, but you will be required to provide an explanation to Airbnb justifying this.

The major potential issue with *Instant Book* is that this feature is often used by people who want to make a last-minute booking in a hurry. That means they may not take the time to read your House Rules or property description carefully and this can lead to an increased risk of cancellations if they later discover, for example, that your check-in time does not fit with their travel plans or they hadn't noted that you don't allow pets. If you plan to use *Instant Book*, it is also important that you remember to keep your calendar up to date. If you forget to note that you will be unavailable and a guest uses *Instant Book* to reserve a night during that period, you will face penalties from Airbnb.

Whether you use this feature or not will depend on how you approach your Airbnb hosting. If you want the maximum Occupancy Rate regardless of potential extra work, *Instant Book* may be for you. If you have less time to spare and you want the time to plan and prepare for each guest in advance, perhaps this feature is not ideal? Remember, you can always test the *Instant Book* feature for your listing and then turn it off if it doesn't work for you. You can also turn this feature on or off according to your availability and during peak or low accommodation demand periods.

ONE NIGHT MINIMUM

Another parameter you must consider for your listing is the minimum length of stay. You can set this as anything from a single night upwards. You can choose different minimums for different days of the week; for example, you can set a two-night minimum for weekends and a one night minimum for weekdays.

The principal benefit of choosing a one night minimum is that you will appeal to the maximum number of potential guests. The problem is that meeting with guests during their arrival and departure and cleaning and reset every day are going to eat into your time and, if you use a management service, cost you more.

One way of mitigating this is to separate the cleaning fee for your property from the rental cost. You have the option when setting your price in Airbnb either to include the cleaning fee in your rental or to make it separate. If you make this a separate charge, it will apply to each booking, regardless of the length of stay. This can help to offset the additional time and/or cost of short stays.

For example, if you charge $50 per night plus a $15 cleaning fee, you will receive $65 per night for one night stays but just $53 per night for five night stays. However, if you do charge a separate cleaning fee, this can deter short-term guests.

Like many other aspects of Airbnb, setting the minimum number of nights depends on your goals and the time you have available. Shorter stays can attract more guests and you may be able to achieve a higher nightly rate, but they will need more work. Decide what works for you and choose the appropriate minimum length of stay and remember that you can always change this later if it isn't working.

ADDITIONAL GUESTS

One mistake that many beginning Airbnb hosts make is to set a price for their property, regardless of the number of guests. If your property can accommodate more than two people, it's better to set a base price which covers two people and then under *'Extra Charges'* add a fee for each additional guest.

This helps to keep your base price low, making your listing look attractive to potential guests and moving it up the search rankings while maximizing your potential profits.

> *Pro-Tip: Options like Instant Booking, minimum length of stay and how you deal with extra guests are very important ways of maximizing the revenue potential of our Airbnb property.*

AIRBNB HOST STATUS

Becoming a Superhost

Airbnb designates some hosts as Superhosts. Being a Superhost places a badge on your listing and brings recognition as a host who is friendly and professional. Potential guests can choose to filter search results to show only Superhosts.

There are clearly benefits to being an Airbnb Superhost, but how do you become one? All Airbnb hosts are eligible to become Superhosts if they meet four criteria;

- ✓ Host a minimum of ten stays in the previous twelve months (or for long-stay accommodation, one hundred nights involving at least three separate stays), and,
- ✓ Receive a minimum review rating of 4.8 for at least 50% of stays, and, or 80% of your reviews must be 5-star.
- ✓ Respond to 90% of new messages within 24 hours, and,
- ✓ Have no cancellations in the previous twelve months unless these were justified to and accepted by Airbnb as not being the fault of the host.

5. Listing your property

Superhost Assessment takes place every three months and, if you meet the criteria, you will automatically become a Superhost. In some countries, Superhosts who have maintained their status for twelve months receive a bonus in the form of a $100 coupon for Airbnb travel. However, if you fail any of the relevant assessment criteria, you will lose your Superhost status, so you need to keep focused on these things.

Being a Superhost is useful because it gives potential guests the assurance that you have some experience, that guests like staying at your property, that you communicate promptly and that you aren't likely to cancel their booking. A proportion of potential guests do use the Superhost filter when searching for an Airbnb listing and Superhosts seem to receive more interest and more bookings than non-Superhost listings, though the difference is actually quite small.

Becoming a Superhost costs nothing and it may bring more bookings. The criteria for becoming a Superhost are things that you should be aiming for anyway as an Airbnb host, so achieving them shouldn't take more time or effort. Superhost status is something every Airbnb host should be working towards.

> *Pro-Tip: Becoming a Superhost is very important and it provides an assurance to potential guests that you have reached a certain standard of hosting. All Airbnb hosts should aim to attain Superhost status as quickly as possible.*

Free tool available:

www.theairbnbplaybook.com/tools

AIRBNB PLUS

In 2018, Airbnb introduced a new feature called Airbnb Plus. According to Airbnb this is a way of identifying Airbnb properties which offer a higher level of accommodation, closer to what a guest might expect from a hotel. Initially Plus was rolled out in a limited number of locations but this service is being introduced in many popular Airbnb locations.

Any Airbnb host can qualify for the Airbnb Plus Program, but they must satisfy a number of requirements. First, they must have hosted at least one stay, must have an average guest rating of 4.8 stars or higher and must have accepted 95 percent of reservations without any last minute last-minute cancellations in the last twelve months. Then the property must meet the requirements of a one-hundred-point checklist. Some of these points are clear and simple to understand, for example;

- Is the property clean, tidy and well maintained?
- Does the property provide a television with access to media entertainment such as Netflix and with a remote control?

However, some of the Plus checklist points are much more subjective. For example;

- Is the home thoughtfully designed and does it reflect the host's personality?
- Does the property have a cohesive interior style?

You can see the full *Airbnb Plus checklist* on the Airbnb site:

https://www.airbnb.com/b/plushomechecklist

If you feel that your property qualifies and meets all the points on the checklist you can apply, and Airbnb will send a third-party inspector to view and photograph your property. It costs $150 to apply for Airbnb Plus.

Airbnb claim that joining Plus gives hosts a number of advantages including better visibility in search results and an assurance for guests that the property

5. Listing your property

has been checked and reviewed by professionals. However, there are some downsides to Plus. For example, the photographs taken during the inspection visit will be used to replace those already in your listing and you will have no control over which image is used as the cover for your listing. You will also no longer be able to change the descriptive text in your listing.

If you already have professional quality photographs and you are happy with your cover image, you may not want to give these up in exchange for Plus status. Currently there is no good data to show whether Plus hosts get more bookings than other Airbnb hosts so this is something that you may want to approach with caution.

AIRBNB COLLECTIONS

An Airbnb Collection is a group of properties highlighted as suitable for a particular type of trip or guest. Potential guests can use these collections to narrow their search for a property so it makes sense to have your property added to a particular collection that will appeal to your target demographic if possible.

The two most popular and significant Collections are Family and Work though there are also more niche Collections featuring properties suitable for honeymoons, for example. Airbnb will automatically add your property to a suitable Collection if it meets certain eligibility requirements.

You can find the Airbnb criteria for joining the Work Collection here:

https://www.airbnb.com/help/article/2186/how-do-i-join-the-work-collection?

and for the Family Collection here:

https://www.airbnb.com/help/article/2187/how-do-i-join-the-family-collection?q=the%20family%20collection.

You can find more general information on Airbnb Collections here:

https://www.airbnb.com/help/article/2185/what-is-a-collection?

TIPS TO MAKE YOUR LISTING STAND OUT

MAKE YOUR LISTING TITLE CATCHY AND KEEP IT UP TO DATE

If there is a major event close to your property, consider updating your title to include this; *'5 mins walk to Comic-Com'* is likely to grab attention in the weeks leading up to an event.

YOUR COVER IMAGE MUST BE ENGAGING

Don't just use a random image – choose your cover image and use something that highlights an unique or interesting feature of your property.

MAKE SURE YOUR HOST PROFILE IS APPEALING

Include a photograph of yourself with a welcoming smile. Tell guests a little about yourself and explain that you are looking forward to meeting them.

TAKE THE TIME TO COMPLETE ALL SECTIONS OF YOUR LISTING

A short or not terribly helpful listing implies that you don't care or won't take the time to provide information for guests. Include information not just about the property but also the surrounding area.

EARTH FRIENDLY AIRBNB

Staying in an Airbnb property rather than a hotel uses fewer resources and has less environmental impact, and this is important to Airbnb guests. A survey carried out by Airbnb in 2017 found that for over 66% of guests, the environmental benefits of home sharing were a factor in their choice of accommodation. Over 90% of Airbnb hosts now incorporate some form of green practice into their hosting.

These things can include;

- Providing environmentally friendly cleaning products, and,
- Providing re-cycling or even composting facilities for use by guests, and,

5. Listing your property

- Using environmentally friendly forms of heating such as solar panels or geothermal heating, and,

- Providing bicycles for guest use and/or encouraging the use of public transportation, and,

- Ensuring that appliances such as washers and dishwashers are energy efficient and have eco-friendly settings, and,

- Providing cloth bags that guests can use while shopping, and,

- If your property is close to cafes, provide re-usable mugs which guests can use.

Unfortunately, Airbnb does not have an *'Eco-Friendly'* badge or even a Collection for green properties, so all you can do at the moment is add these things to your property description and, if you have an important eco-friendly feature, mention this in your listing title.

> *Pro-Tip: Data shows that Airbnb guests are particularly concerned about the environmental impact of travel and accommodation – use your listing to emphasize the green credentials of your property to increase the listings attractiveness and your occupancy rates.*

ADVERTISING YOUR PROPERTY ON OTHER PLATFORMS

You can share your Airbnb listing through different social media platforms or your own website by using the *Manage Listings* function on Airbnb. Using this it is possible to share your listing on Facebook, Instagram, Pinterest, Google+ or Twitter or to embed your listing in your website. More information on this function can be found here.

If your area has tourist information websites, you can also promote your listing on these and if you can find bloggers covering travel and accommodation in your area, why not reach out to see if they will feature your property?

Be creative – share your listing in as many places as possible and, if you don't already have a website, why not create one specifically to promote your property?

SEO FOR YOUR AIRBNB LISTING

When a potential guest searches Airbnb, they use a dedicated search engine. This is similar in some ways to Internet search engines such as Google, but it uses its own metrics and algorithms to decide what to show and how to rank results.

As an Airbnb host, you want your listing to appear as high as possible in any search results and to do this you need to consider Search Engine Optimization (SEO) for your listing.

One of the most important ways to ensure you appear high on the list of search results is to have guest review ratings that are as high as possible. Airbnb want to encourage guests to stay at properties that have high ratings because they are more likely to be happy and to continue to use the Airbnb service. So, Airbnb will put properties with high guest ratings above other similar properties when search results are displayed. Make sure your guest reviews are positive (you will find more about the Airbnb Reviews process in the next chapter).

When a potential guest sees your listing in the search results, they can see both your title and the photograph you have chosen to be your cover image. Both need to be sufficiently engaging to make potential guests want to look at your listing in more detail.

Other than for promoting properties which have good review scores, Airbnb do not publicize the algorithms or metrics they use to organize search results. However, the experiences of other Airbnb hosts suggest that the following may help to improve the SEO of your listing;

- **Log in to Airbnb profile regularly.** Airbnb tracks your log-in activity and uses this to assess your availability to guests. Frequent log-ins may help to boost search rankings.

5. Listing your property

- **Keep your Calendar up to date.** Just like your log-in activity, Airbnb monitors how often you update your calendar. The more updates the better. If you don't have any bookings to update, you can cheat by blocking in a date or dates in the future and then later unblocking them.

- **Turn on Instant Book.** Airbnb are keen to promote the flexibility of instant booking and turning this feature on may increase your search ranking.

- **Relax your cancellation policy.** Airbnb are keen to promote hosts with the *Flexible* cancellation policy.

- **Delete your maximum stay limit.** Anecdotal evidence suggests that deleting a maximum stay length may improve search ranking, but be aware of potential problems with guests who acquire tenants' rights – more about this in the next chapter.

- **Ensure your title and description include important keywords.** Use the Airbnb *Search* function for your area using an address or area. As you type you will see a list of popular search terms for that area. Look at these carefully – they are a useful guide to what potential guests are searching for. Are there terms, locations, events or areas that seem to be popular – if so, consider adding these to your title or description.

These things may give a small boost to your search ranking, but the most important things that will make your listing stand out and appear high on the search results are good review scores plus an engaging title and cover image.

GOOGLE ADWORDS

Google offers a service called Adwords which allows you to show an advertisement to potential buyers and you will be charged only if someone clicks on to your advertisement. You can set your own budget and this can be a very cost-effective way of reaching potential customers. But, is this something that can help Airbnb hosts?

First of all, Airbnb already use advertisements which appear in Google for anyone searching for accommodation. This applies to certain markets only and, if applicable, your property will be enrolled in this scheme automatically unless you opt out through your Airbnb account. If you receive a booking through someone clicking on a Google ad, the hosting fee will be increased slightly to cover the cost of the advertisement.

Given that, is it worth using Google Adwords to provide additional views for your Airbnb listing? That rather depends on how your listing is performing. If you have already optimized your Airbnb listing using the guidance provided here but you still aren't achieving the Occupancy Rate you are looking for, perhaps a service like Google Adwords may help? Alternatively, perhaps it might be better to simply reduce your prices to generate more interest?

Opinion on the usefulness of Adwords is divided amongst Airbnb hosts. Some use it, many feel that it is a waste of money unless you have something very unique to advertise. You can find more information about Google Adwords here.

USING LOCAL TRAVEL AND BOOKING SITES

Airbnb hosts may be able to use local travel and tourism agencies and sites to increase bookings. This is especially applicable to hosts who choose to participate in the Airbnb *Experiences* scheme where hosts use their local knowledge to offer guests access to activities, they might not otherwise be able to experience. This can involve anything from undertaking cooking or art classes with a host to outdoor activities or even guided tours of local landmarks.

Offering these sorts of activities may help to encourage guests and it may allow you to link with a local tourist agency who will promote your listing through their site. In the UK, for example, the National tourist agency, *Visit Britain*, announced in 2019 that they will be partnering with Airbnb to promote Experiences across the UK.

Contact your local tourist agency and find out whether they would be willing to promote your property and consider experiences for your guests which might make this more attractive.

5. Listing your property

CHAPTER 5 KEY POINTS

- ✓ Complete your Airbnb Host Profile, potential quests picks hosts with complete profiles above ones with no profile.

- ✓ Create a title, description and photographs for your listing and think about how to make your listing stand out. Look at your competitions listings before completing these steps.

- ✓ Set your cancellation policy and make it as relaxed as possible to encourage bookings.

- ✓ Enable Instant Booking.

- ✓ Set minimum length of stay at 2 days during high season and to 1 day during low seasons.

- ✓ Decide whether you want to work towards becoming a Superhost, join Airbnb Plus or have your property in a Airbnb Collection.

- ✓ Take high quality photographs of your listing, it makes a big difference.

- ✓ Think about making your Airbnb earth and ecofriendly to set it apart from the competition.

- ✓ Think about how you can optimize your Airbnb listing's SEO on Airbnb and on other platforms.

- ✓ Consider advertising on other platforms especially in slow season.

6
RUNNING
YOUR PROPERTY

6. Running the Property

Dealing with guests is the heart of any successful Airbnb business. You can have the most beautiful property available, but you also need to know how to keep your guests happy if you want to build a successful Airbnb business. That's what this chapter is about – how to deal with guests in such a way that they will become satisfied customers who will give you 5 Star reviews.

RECEIVING BOOKINGS AND COMMUNICATIONS

The first contact you will have with a potential guest is when they send a message through Airbnb to make a booking or to ask a question. Your response to this initial contact is very important.

- **Respond promptly**. No-one wants to wait long for a response and a potential guest may have contacted several hosts – if you are the first to respond, you may get the booking. Always try to respond within 24 hours and more quickly if possible (and remember that, if you want to become a Superhost, you must respond to at least 90% of messages within 24 hours).

- **Keep it Short**. Your initial message should be no longer than 100 words and shorter if possible. Your potential guest can see all the information they need about the property on your listing and in your house rules.

- **Be polite and take the time to answer all questions**. Guests may have all sorts of unexpected questions about your property and/or the area. Try to answer these fully or ask for more time to find out if you don't know the answer. Always be courteous and never use terms or language that might be offensive.

- **Keep your Airbnb Calendar up to date**. Nothing will irritate a potential guest more than making a booking and then finding that the property isn't available because you forgot to update your Calendar.

Free tool available:

www.theairbnbplaybook.com/tools

You may receive messages from guests asking for a discounted rate. Whether you accept this or not is up to you. If you have a low Occupancy Rate, offering a small discount may be a good way to fill a quiet period. If the enquiry comes in some time before the booking date, you can suggest that the person checks back one week prior to the booking – if it is still vacant, you may then want to consider a discount. One of the advantages of Airbnb is that pricing is completely flexible and entirely up to you – if you want to offer a discount, that's fine. If you don't, you won't be penalized by Airbnb.

Once a booking is confirmed there are several other messages that you will want to send to guests. These will include as a minimum;

- **Booking Confirmation.** A confirmation that the booking has been received and approved by the host.

- **Check-in and Check-out Information.** Details of when, where and how guests will check-in including contact telephone numbers or other essential information. You may also want to include a copy of your House Rules here.

- **Review Reminder.** A polite request sent after check-out asking your guests to complete a review of your property.

Fortunately, the content and sending of these and other messages can be automated to save time – this is discussed in more detail in Chapter 8.

PREPARING FOR GUESTS TO ARRIVE

Before your guests arrive, there are several things that you will want to do or to check. It may be helpful to create a checklist for your property - here are some items you may want to include.

CLEANING

Whether you have done it yourself or sub-contracted to someone else, check that all tiled floors have been mopped, all carpets have been vacuumed, everything in the bathroom is clean, that the kitchen and all appliances and worktops are clean and that all bins have been emptied.

BEDDING AND TOWELS

Make sure that all bedding and towels are fresh and make sure that there are spare towels and bedding as well as extra pillows available for guests.

KITCHEN

Make sure that there is adequate kitchen roll, cleaning supplies and clean drying cloths. If applicable, make sure that there are supplies of dishwasher liquid/tablets and detergent. Check the fridge to make sure that it is clean and that previous guests haven't left any food behind. Check that condiments, olive oil and sugar are present in sufficient quantity. Check that all required cutlery, plates, cups, mugs, glasses and pots and pans are present, in good order and clean.

BATHROOM

Check that there is toilet roll, soap, shampoo and conditioner.

OTHER ITEMS

If you provide a welcome basket for guests and/or beverages make sure that these are replenished. Make sure that there are spare trash bags and light bulbs. Ensure that a copy of your House Manual is available with a local map and sufficient copies of any relevant brochures or other information about the local area. Make sure that your first-aid kit is fully stocked and that all smoke/fire detectors are operational.

DE-CLUTTER!

Make sure that all areas are tidy and that your items or items left by previous guests are safely removed.

> *Pro-Tip: Make sure your property has a pleasant aroma when guests arrive by providing air-fresheners, pot-pourri, fresh-cut flowers or using an aromatherapy spray.*

WELCOMING GUESTS

Image; Airbnb Media Resources

First impressions are important and providing the personal touch can get your guests' stay off to a great start. Of course, it is possible to arrange for your guests to securely pick up keys without the need for you to be present, but if you can, it's always better to personally meet your Airbnb guests.

Your guests will have travelled to your property, they may be tired and they may not know the area, so a friendly face showing them round and answering any questions will be very welcome.

One point that is commonly noted in positive Airbnb reviews is *'host helpfulness'* and many Airbnb hosts note that when they meet with guests, they tend to receive higher review scores. This also means that if there are quirky things about your property that are difficult to explain in writing, you will have the opportunity to explain these in person.

Don't overstay your welcome – your guests will want to get settled in as soon as possible so, once you have handed over the keys, shown them around, confirmed that they understand the check-out arrangements and have your contact information and you have asked if they have any questions, leave them to settle in.

6. Running the Property

If you don't have the time to personally meet your guests, there are specialist management services who will do this for you. For example, companies such as Evolve in the US and Hostmaker in Europe provide this service as do many other companies – just Google *'Airbnb management service'* to find management companies in your area who will meet with guests on your behalf.

DEALING WITH ISSUES DURING GUEST STAYS AND COMMUNICATIONS DURING THEIR STAY

Life doesn't always go as planned and, no matter how carefully you prepare, it is virtually certain that some of your guests will experience issues during their stay. You can't always avoid these things happening, but your response to guest issues is a critical part of ensuring that your review scores stay high.

- **Be available!** Nothing will make your guests more unhappy than if they can't contact you if they have a problem. If you have given your guests a contact telephone number or email, make sure that you are available and/or check regularly for guest messages.

- **Be prepared.** What are you going to do if an appliance in your property fails during a guest stay, or if the plumbing needs urgent attention or if the guests can't operate your keyless entry system? Some issues you will be able to deal with yourself but think in advance about things like having contact numbers for emergency plumbers/electricians/locksmiths and having the information about appliance guarantees to hand so that you can organize replacement or repair as quickly as possible.

- **Listen to your guests.** Always make your guests feel that you are taking their issues seriously. Even if you feel these are trivial, they matter to your guests or they wouldn't have bothered contacting you. Tell them you understand why they are unhappy and what you are going to do to try to resolve the issue.

- **Keep talking.** If you are talking to specialists about fixing an issue, let guests know what is happening and when the issue is likely to be resolved.

If you can't fix the problem right away, can you help ameliorate it? For example, if the central heating boiler in your property develops a fault that will take several days to fix, can you offer to provide portable heaters as a short-term solution? If the shower in your property has a problem, are there communal showers in the area to which your guests could have access?

- **Sorry is not the hardest word.** If something does go wrong, an apology from you will go a long way towards preventing a negative review. The problem may not directly be your fault, but as a host you are responsible for your guest's stay so apologizing if things haven't gone as planned is just good manners.

- **Making up for it.** If an issue has negatively impacted a guest stay, consider offering some form of recompense. This could take the form of an offer of a partial refund of their payment or an offer to pay for a meal in a local restaurant or providing a basket of food, wine or other goodies to the guests.

The future commercial success of your Airbnb business depends on good reviews so it's worth going the extra distance to keep guests happy if they have problems. Do this right and when the time comes for them to write a review, they won't focus on the problem but on your helpful response.

> *Pro-Tips: No matter how careful your preparation and planning, things will go wrong. However, that is less important than how you respond to problems. If there are problems but you deal with them promptly and politely, you can keep your guests happy and your reviews positive.*

6. Running the Property

HOW TO DEAL WITH GUESTS WHO WON'T LEAVE

In many parts of the world, a tenant who stays in a property for 30 days or more may become eligible for certain rights which mean that it is difficult for you to eject them even if they don't pay rent. Fortunately, this is very unusual on Airbnb rentals, but you should be aware of how to identify and avoid such potential squatters.

- **Know the law.** The 30-day period is not set in stone – in some areas, local or national laws may have a longer or shorter period before a person becomes eligible for tenants' rights. Find out what the statutes are in your area.

- **Don't allow Instant Book for stays that will give tenants' rights.** Find out how long people have to stay in a property in your area before they become eligible for tenants' rights. Turn off Instant Booking for anything including and over this length of time.

- **Scrutinize the guest.** If you get a request for a longer booking, scrutinize it even more carefully than usual. Does the potential guest have reviews and a history on Airbnb? Have they verified their identity? If the answer is no, this could be a potential problem.

- **Do a credit check.** For longer stays, it may be worth doing a credit check on your potential guest. You will have to ask their permission and get additional information. A potential squatter is unlikely to share this information with you or to have a good credit record.

- **Don't do a deal outside Airbnb!** Some potential squatters may offer to pay you outside Airbnb. Don't be tempted to do this – if you deal with a tenant outside Airbnb you will lose the support that Airbnb can provide and access to things like the *Host Guarantee.*

Guest who won't leave are very, very rare on Airbnb, but if you follow this guidance, you can be certain this won't happen to you.

THE CHECK-OUT PROCESS

Your check-out requirements should be clearly set out in your House Manual. Will you be present or can guests check-out on their own? You may also want to put a notice by the door confirming what you want guests to do before they leave. Each property will be different, but these are some of the things that you may want to include in your check-our procedure;

- What time is check-out?

- Where should the keys be left and should the property be locked?

- Do you expect guests to clean kitchens, bathrooms or other areas and/or take the trash out?

- Do you expect guests to strip beds and leave the bedding somewhere specific?

- Do you want guests to turn down or off heating, hot water or A/C before they leave ?

- Can guests leave luggage and collect it later? Explain how this works.

- Remind guests to be sure they haven't left anything behind.

- Do you want guests to call, text or send a message to note they are leaving?

It's always good to end these check-out instructions by thanking guests for their stay, a hope that they have enjoyed themselves and to wish them safe onward travel.

THE AIRBNB REVIEW PROCESS

Reviews are central to Airbnb. Your reviews as a host will influence your ranking in search results and will be one of the main things that potential guests read before deciding if they want to stay with you. Your reviews of your guests are also important because these are how other hosts will evaluate these potential customers.

6. Running the Property

As a host, you need to understand how the review process works. Every guest who stays with you will be invited to leave a *Review*. This review can be up to 1,000 words in length and will be visible to everyone who uses Airbnb. Guests also have the option to leave *Private Feedback* – that's a post-stay message that is visible only to the host. Reviews include *Star Ratings* – a quick summary of how guests rate various aspects of their stay with 1 star the worst and 5 stars the best. If you have a rating of three stars or more and you have received at least three reviews, this will appear on your listing. To become a Superhost, you must have a rating of 4.8 or higher. If you cancel a reservation, an automated *Cancellation Review* will appear on your listing and profile. These can't be removed or avoided if a host cancels a booking. Star Ratings are given in six areas:

- Cleanliness
- Accuracy
- Communication
- Check-in
- Value
- Location

A host's overall rating for a particular stay is calculated by taking an average of these six scores to produce an Overall Experience rating. A host's overall rating score is calculated by taking an average of all Overall Experience ratings.

A guest or host has up to 14 days to leave a review. The review will not be publicly visible until the corresponding guest or host has also posted a review, or, the 14 day review period has passed. This means that you can't wait until you have seen the review a guest has left before you review them and that your Host Review will be made public whether or not you review the guest. Reviews can be edited for up to 48 hours after posting or until the corresponding guest/host leaves a review. After that, they cannot be edited.

Your guests don't have to leave a review or rating, but as a host, you want to have as many positive reviews as possible. One way to encourage guests to leave a review is to send them a message a few days after their stay. This may take the form of;

> *'Thank you for being a guest. I hope you enjoyed your stay? Your opinion matters and positive reviews are very helpful. I would be most grateful if you would take a few moments to complete a review of your stay in Airbnb. If there is anything that you felt could be improved, I'd appreciate this information through the private feedback section.'*

RESPONDING TO AIRBNB REVIEWS

Reviews only become visible on Airbnb if one of two conditions are met; either both the guest and the host must have left a review, or, if either has left a review and fourteen days have passed without the other leaving a review. The reason for this is to avoid *'tit-for-tat'* reviews where either a guest or host leaves a bad review and the other responds by leaving a bad review as retaliation.

As a host, this means that you cannot see your guest's review until you have completed and posted a review of that guest, or until the fourteen days period in which you can leave a review has passed. If you don't leave a review, your guest's review will become visible to you and everyone else on Airbnb after fourteen days, but you cannot then leave a review of the guest because the review period has expired.

However, in all circumstances you can respond to a guest review by leaving a comment which can be seen by all Airbnb users.

The policy of Airbnb is that no reviews are removed unless they violate the *Airbnb review content guidelines* *(https://www.airbnb.com/help/article/546/what-is-airbnb-s-content-policy)* which prohibit things like discriminatory comments or the inclusion of personally identifying information. However, as a host, you do have the option to respond to guest reviews. If you receive a negative review, you should respond by explaining how you have addressed the problem the guest experienced without being confrontational or rude. However,

6. Running the Property

it also good to respond to positive reviews – a quick note thanking the guest and noting that you appreciate their taking the time to post a review shows that you are an engaged and attentive host.

If you cancel a booking and you receive an automated Cancellation Review, respond and explain why the booking was cancelled.

Airbnb reviews are shown on your listing in the order in which the stays occurred. So, if you do get a negative review, the best thing you can do is address the problem and ensure that it is followed by positive reviews. That way, when a potential guest looks at your listing they will see the negative review as old news and will be aware that subsequent guests have been happy.

DON'T GET INTO ARGUMENTS

Even if you are unhappy with a review, don't criticize the guest in your response. It's fine to note that, for example, you are surprised when a guest complains about a lack of some gadget or amenity which is clearly noted in your listing, but always be professional, polite and adult in your responses. If a guest raises a legitimate concern, use your response to describe how you are going to deal with the issue. No-one is going to want to stay with a host who appears defensive or confrontational!

REVIEWING GUESTS

As a host, you will have the opportunity to review your guests. This is the resource other hosts will use to assess this person as a potential guest. Be honest here, but keep it short, professional and polite. Hopefully, most of your guests will get positive reviews, so you can create a standard template you can use for guest reviews like;

> 'Great guest(s), good communications, respected my house rules and a pleasure to host. I would be delighted to host this guest/these guests again and I would recommend them to any other Airbnb host without reservation.'

LEARN FROM YOUR NEGATIVE REVIEWS

No-one wants to get a bad review whether it is public or through Private Feedback, but this information can help you improve as an Airbnb host. Ask yourself;

- Could the issue have been avoided by changing or providing more detailed information in your listing?

- Is there something that you can do to prevent the issue from re-occurring?

- Is there something in your check-in, check-out, cleaning or re-set processes that can be changed to avoid the issue?

> *Pro-Tip: Learn from both positive and negative reviews and use these to maintain and improve your Airbnb hosting.*

5 STAR REVIEW CHECKLIST

Your aim should always be to get a 5 Star review rating. Written reviews are useful, but the star rating is what potential guests will see in search results. To make sure you get a 5 Star rating, consider each area you are rated on;

- **Cleanliness.** Every guest wants to feel that their accommodation is clean and fresh. Look at your property critically – is there anything shabby or worn that could be improved or are there areas that could be cleaner? Have any guests mentioned a lack of cleanliness or marked you down in the past? Address these issues if you want five stars in this area.

- **Accuracy.** Is your listing an accurate description of your property? Of course, you want the listing to be as attractive as possible, but perhaps it's better to underplay a little? A guest who is pleasantly surprised is much more likely to give a 5 star ranking.

- **Communication.** This is simple – respond promptly to all requests for booking or other guest enquiries and ensure you are available while guests are staying.

6. Running the Property

- **Check-in.** Be there on-time, make sure that guests know their way around the property and answer any questions your guests may have. Don't leave until guests seem happy and settled.

- **Value.** This is subjective and most guests won't book with you unless they feel that you are offering value. What you can do is offer little extras like beverages, a welcome basket and other small things that make guests feel that they are getting something extra.

- **Location.** This is the most difficult section in which to score 5 Stars – after all, you can't improve the location of your property. What you can do is provide in the description as much information as possible– for example, how far is it to walk/drive to public transportation, shops, restaurant and bars? Be honest and accurate and if guests do mark you down in this area, try to find out why and update your listing accordingly.

Free tool available:

www.theairbnbplaybook.com/tools

USE YOUR REVIEWS TO BOOST YOUR RATINGS

If your ratings aren't reaching the standards you want, read them carefully to assess what you need to do to improve. If this isn't clear, send guests a polite message asking them what they would like to see improved.

The best way to achieve positive reviews and high ratings is to listen to feedback from your guests and react. Improve where you can, add to the description in your listing where necessary to ensure that guests know what to expect before they arrive and even consider dropping your prices if guests complain about value.

To be a successful Airbnb host, you need good reviews and ratings so this is something you must stay focused on.

THE DREADED 4 STAR RATING

One issue with the Airbnb star rating system is that you need around 75% of guests to leave overall 5 Star ratings for you to become a Superhost. However, 4 Stars represents *'Good'* so, a guest leaving you an overall 4 Star rating may feel that this is a positive review. In Airbnb terms, 4 Stars just isn't enough and if every guest rates every part of their stay as *'Good'*, that might mean an awful lot of satisfied customers, but it won't allow you to become a Superhost. If you get enough 4 Star reviews, Airbnb may even contact you to suggest that you need to make improvements!

The problem lies with the Airbnb Star rating system itself. If most people are asked to rate any experience from one to five stars, they are probably going to choose 3 Stars (*'Okay'*) or 4 Stars (*'Good'*) if the experience simply lives up to their expectations. Most people won't choose 5 Stars (*'Excellent'*) unless the experience delivers significantly more than they expected. Most hotels are very happy with four star reviews. If you get consistent 4 Star reviews on Airbnb, you will never become a Superhost.

How can you avoid 4 Star reviews and encourage guests to leave you 5 Star reviews? Some hosts have found that explaining the Airbnb Star rating system to guests can help. If you send out a message after a guest checks-out, thanking them for their stay and reminding them to leave a review, you may want to consider adding something like the following;

> *We appreciate your feedback and review and we always strive to provide 5 Star service. You may not be aware that the Airbnb rating system means that a 4 Star rating is regarded as poor, even though it is listed as 'Good'. Four star reviews negatively impact our overall rating.*
>
> *If you were happy with your stay, may I ask that you give us a 5 Star rating to help us maintain our listing?*
>
> *Thank you so much!*

6. Running the Property

Some hosts feel that asking for a 5 Star review is crass, but if guests don't understand how the rating system works, they are likely to give you 3 or 4 Stars, and that just isn't good enough. Nothing is more frustrating for a host than receiving a glowing written review accompanied by 4 Star ratings.

You can also put a similar message in the printed copy of your House Rules. There is no guarantee that your guests will read this or a message or that they will leave you 5 Star reviews if they do, but explaining how the rating system works may help to avoid the dreaded 4 Stars.

CHAPTER 6 KEY POINTS

- ✓ Respond promptly to guest communications, this is a key factor in reaching Super Host status.

- ✓ Make sure your property is clean and fully stocked before quests arrive. Use professional cleaners if your budget allows.

- ✓ Deal promptly with issues during guest stays and remain friendly, courteous and avoid arguments.

- ✓ Make sure you are familiar with the law in your area regarding potential squatters.

- ✓ Understand the review process and how to use it to improve your business.

- ✓ Know how to attain 5 Star reviews and how to avoid 4 Stars. Asks guests to leave a 5-Star review.

7

CLEANING & RESET

7. Cleaning and reset

Cleaning and re-stocking your property between guest stays is something that is going to take time and getting this consistently right is something you need to do if you are going to get those good reviews and ratings. There are four different ways of doing the cleaning and re-set for your property;

- Do it yourself, or,
- Sub-contract to an individual, or,
- Sub-contract to a specialist cleaning company, or,
- Sub-contract to a Property Management Company.

Using a Property Management Company is discussed in detail later in this chapter and there are pros and cons to each of the other options.

DOING IT YOURSELF OR GETTING HELP?
DOING YOUR OWN CLEANING AND RE-SET

Pros

- Maximizes your profits.
- You are not reliant on anyone else.
- The cleaning gets done the way that you want.

Cons

- Time. Cleaning and re-set take time. Probably more time than you anticipate. If you set a one-night minimum, you could be doing this every day, between one guests' departure and another's arrival. Do you have the time and availability to do this? Would the time you do have be better spent finding ways to improve and grow your Airbnb business?

EMPLOYING AN INDIVIDUAL CLEANER

Pros

- You save time.
- You can build a relationship with your cleaner.
- You can train your cleaner to do things the way you want.

Cons

- Costs more than doing it yourself.
- Single point of failure. If your cleaner is sick or can't attend for any reason, you have a problem.
- Who are you employing? If you use a cleaning company or management service, they will perform background checks before any staff enter your property. Can you do the same? Can you follow-up references?
- You need flexibility. Your booking may be for several days or a single night and may be booked weeks in advance or at 24 hours notice. Is your cleaner able to respond to your changing requirements?

SUB-CONTRACTING TO A SPECIALIST CLEANING COMPANY

Pros

- Flexibility. A cleaning company will have access to staff. This means that you aren't dependent on the availability of a single person and there is a better chance of a positive response to short-term requests.
- Insurance. Professional cleaners working for a specialist company will be covered by that company's insurance in case of damage.

Cons

- Costs more than doing it yourself or employing an individual cleaner.
- You won't always get the same cleaner so the standard of cleaning may vary.

7. Cleaning and reset

Deciding which approach is best for you means thinking about how much time you have and deciding if you want to do your own cleaning? You can always start out doing this and then consider switching to employing a cleaner or using a cleaning service once you start to pick up bookings.

CLEANING AND RE-SET CHECKLIST

Whether you will do your own cleaning or pay someone else to do it, creating a cleaning and re-set checklist for your property is a good way of making sure that nothing gets missed. This checklist will be unique to your property, but it should include;

- ✓ Areas to be tidied, dusted, swept, mopped and vacuumed,
- ✓ Bins to be emptied,
- ✓ Bathroom items to be cleaned including mirror, toilet, sink, bidet, shower, bath, etc.,
- ✓ Kitchen items to be checked and cleaned including oven, microwave, fridge, dishwasher, sink, worktops, washing machine, etc.,
- ✓ Check that all cutlery, plates, cups, pots, pans, etc. are present and properly washed-up,
- ✓ Change bedding, towels, bathmats, drying cloths, cleaning ., items, etc.,
- ✓ Re-stock any consumables including beverages, condiments, toilet roll, kitchen roll, shampoo, soap, etc.,
- ✓ Check all appliances, lights, heaters and smoke detectors are working correctly,
- ✓ Guest final touches – flowers, chocolate, a welcome basket, etc.

Having a checklist is helpful if you are doing your own cleaning because it makes it less likely that you'll forget something, and it's very useful if you want someone else to know what you expect to be done. This is good if you decide to use a cleaner or cleaning service but, even if you intend to do your own cleaning it can be helpful because if you get sick or can't do the cleaning for any reason, a checklist makes it easier to hand over to someone else.

HOW LONG WILL CLEANING TAKE?

One of the most common questions that beginner Airbnb hosts ask is; how long will it take to clean my property? This is important because it lets you understand if you will have the time to do this yourself or if you need to employ help.

Unfortunately, there is no easy answer. Each property is different and the cleaning standards of each host are also different so there is no simple algorithm that tells you that a certain number of square feet will take a fixed amount of time to clean properly.

To find out how long it will take to clean your property; do it. Start from scratch and clean it precisely as you would if you were expecting a guest (this is also a good way to make sure that your checklist covers everything). How long did it take? Accepting that repetition may make things a little faster, that's around how long it will take to clean your property to your standards.

Most hosts are surprised to find that cleaning and re-set take longer than they expect. Even cleaning and preparing the smallest apartment to the standard that a guest will expect can take two hours or more. When you are planning your Airbnb business, plan for this and assess whether you really have the time to do this yourself? If not, you're going to need to use a cleaner, a cleaning service or even a property management service and this will impact your profitability.

> *Pro-Tip: Cleanliness is one of the criteria used in achieving an overall 5 Star rating and one of the issues which most often leads to complaints by guests. Making sure your property is always clean and fresh is essential to running a successful Airbnb business.*

7. Cleaning and reset

USING A PROPERTY MANAGEMENT SERVICE?

Running all aspects of your own Airbnb maximizes your profits but takes time and effort. You will be the marketer, scheduler, receptionist, cleaner and perhaps also the emergency contact, handyman and repair person for your business. How much of your time this will take depends on the size and Occupancy Rate of your property. Some hosts say that running a full-time Airbnb will take at least eight hours per week. Others claim twenty or more hours. Do you have that kind of time to spare?

If you don't, there is an option; you can subcontract some or all the tasks associated with renting out your Airbnb property to a short-term rental property management company. Property Management service companies have been around for a long time, but they were traditionally involved in long-term commercial or residential rentals. With the growth of Airbnb and other short-term rental platforms, there are now a number of Management Companies which specialize in short-term rentals.

These companies can take over aspects of your Airbnb rental business including taking bookings and responding to enquiries from guests, handling check-in and check-out, dealing with guest issues during their stay and organizing cleaning and re-set. These companies can take on most of the work that you would otherwise have to do yourself, but of course they require payment for this which will impact your profits. You need to decide whether you have the time to do the management work yourself or whether you can afford to sub-contract aspects to a specialist management company.

Management companies range from Full-Service Rental Property services which will manage every aspect of your Airbnb business on your behalf to specialists who let you outsource some aspects.

How can you find a Property Management service in your area? Sites like *Rented.com (https://www.rented.com/)* can help you find a professional full-service property management service in most major Airbnb markets world-wide. In North America, major providers include;

- *Evolve (https://evolvevacationrental.com/)* Vacation Rental Management cover most of North America,

- *Vacasa (https://www.vacasa.com/)* cover 17 US States,

- *My VR Host (https://www.myvrhost.com/)* cover a number of US States,

- *Pillow (https://www.pillow.com/)* covers California.

These aren't the only options – there are now a number of local and national rental management companies across the US – just Google *'vacation rental management'* to find more. Most base their services on a percentage of your rental charge and this can vary from 10% to 20% or more depending on what you want these companies to do.

Outside the US, there are many more to choose from;

- *Hostmaker (https://hostmaker.com/)* cover several European countries,

- *Guest Ready (https://www.guestready.com/)* cover some European countries in addition to Malaysia, Singapore and Hong Kong,

- *Mister Suite (https://www.mistersuite.com/)* cover properties in Japan.

These are examples only – search for vacation rental property management companies in your area to find many more. As the Airbnb market matures, more and more management companies are offering full-service management of short-term rentals.

Using a full-service management company can be a great way of saving time, but of course their fees will reduce your profits. If you have a single property you let out from time to time, you may be able to keep on top of everything yourself. If you have a property that is fully booked or several properties, it may make sense to outsource to a full-service company.

However, you may not want to outsource every aspect of your Airbnb management, you might just want help with certain aspects. There are also solutions that can help with this;

Guesty (https://www.guesty.com/), for example, don't just provide software to

7. Cleaning and reset

help automate tasks like scheduling cleaning, they also allow you to outsource all your Airbnb communications meaning that you will never lose a booking because you aren't available to respond to a message or because a competitor got there first.

You may want to outsource part of the management of your Airbnb property. For example, you may want to handle check-in and out yourself, but have someone else deal with responding to emergencies. You may want to do the cleaning yourself but have someone else look after repairs and maintaining the garden. Most vacation rental management service providers offer a degree of flexibility – talk to them and explain your requirements. You should be able to negotiate something less than full-service management for a reduced percentage of your booking fee.

Whether or not you decide to use a management company for some, or all of the tasks associated with running your Airbnb rental depends on how much time you have to spare. Doing everything yourself will maximize your profits but takes lots of time. What do you do if you get sick or have an unexpected problem which means that you suddenly don't have the time to spare? Using a management company will reduce your profits but give you flexibility and more time. You need to decide what's right for you.

Free tool available:

www.theairbnbplaybook.com/tools

CHAPTER 7 KEY POINTS

- ✓ Create a cleaning and re-set checklist to standardize the process.

- ✓ Make sure that the cleaning and re-set process is done properly and inspect the apartment afterwards. A clean and neat listing is key in getting a good rating.

- ✓ If you have time constraints sub-contract the cleaning and reset of the apartment, it is worth the cost.

- ✓ Consider using a management service to run the entire property if profitability is sufficient.

8

USEFUL TOOLS & BONUS CONTENT

8. Useful tools and Bonus Content

In this chapter you will find useful contact information for Airbnb, a handy listing of useful links and the tools mentioned in this book, guidance on writing Airbnb reviews and advice on streamlining, automating and improving your Airbnb business.

CONTACTING AIRBNB

TELEPHONE

If you have an urgent need to contact Airbnb, telephone is the best way.

In the US, the Airbnb toll-free customer service number is;

1-855-424-7262

In the UK the Airbnb customer service telephone number is;

02033 181 111

You can find a list of other contact telephone numbers at the Airbnb *Help Center (https://www.airbnb.com/help/contact_us)* on the *How to Contact Airbnb – Customer Service Number* page. However, to access this you will first need to create an Airbnb account – to do this, just click the *'Sign Up'* button and follow the instructions. If you already have an Airbnb account, use the *'Log In'* button to access the Help Center.

EMAIL

You can't directly email Airbnb. The main recommended method of messaging Airbnb is via their *Help Center.* You can use the *'Contact Us'* button in the bottom left of the screen to send a message. To access this service, you will need to be signed in to your Airbnb account.

You will then see a listing of your current bookings. If your question relates to one of these, use the *'Send a Message'* option.

If your question does not relate directly to a booking, click the *'My question is about something else'* option. You will then be asked whether your question is about hosting, a reservation or travelling. If you check the *'Hosting'* option, you will then see a drop-down menu with possible topics for your message which take you to articles in the *Help* archive. If none of these are appropriate, choose the

'Something else' option and you will finally be able to send an email to Airbnb.

TWITTER

Airbnb have dedicated staff who monitor the company Twitter feeds. To contact Airbnb in this way, log into Twitter and search for @Airbnbhelp. Select the 'Follow' option. Send a Direct Message describing your question (doing it this way ensures that your message is private).

MAIL

The primary Airbnb mail address is:

888 Brannan St.

Floor 4

San Francisco, CA 94117

USEFUL LINKS

- *Airbnb Help Center (https://www.airbnb.com/help/)*

- *Responsible Hosting in the US (https://www.airbnb.com/help/article/1376/responsible-hosting-in-the-united-states)* – official Airbnb listing of regulatory requirements for Airbnb hosts in many US Cities.

- *Airbnb Hosting Courses at Udemy (https://www.udemy.com/topic/airbnb-hosting/)*. On-line learning centre which hosts a number of courses for Airbnb hosts. Not officially affiliated with Airbnb.

- *Learn Airbnb (https://learnairbnb.com/blog/)*. A blog site for Airbnb hosts which provides guidance and access to a forum. Not officially affiliated with Airbnb.

- *Get Paid for Your Pad (https://getpaidforyourpad.com/)*. Blog site which includes and podcasts providing guidance for Airbnb hosts. Not officially affiliated with Airbnb.

- *Laptop Landlord (https://laptoplandlord.com/airbnb-tips-for-hosts/)*. Site which provides guidance for Airbnb hosts. Not officially affiliated with Airbnb.

8. Useful tools and Bonus Content

- *The Abundant Host (http://theabundanthost.com/)*. Site which provides guidance and guides for Airbnb hosts. Not officially affiliated with Airbnb.

- *Evolve (https://evolvevacationrental.com/)*. US Vacation Rental Management company.

- *Hostmaker (https://hostmaker.com/)*. European Vacation Rental Management company.

- *Yourwelcome (https://www.yourwelcome.com/)*. Provider of tablets and apps for Airbnb hosts.

USEFUL TOOLS

- *AirDNA (https://www.airdna.co/)* A web app which provides metrics and data for people running Airbnb properties.

- *AirGMS (https://www.airgms.com/)* A web-based service which allows the automation of a number of Airbnb functions.

- *Beyond Pricing (https://beyondpricing.com/)* An on-line service which automatically updates the price of your Airbnb rental to the optimum level.

- *Guesty (https://www.guesty.com/)* A service which allows the automation of many Airbnb tasks as well as supporting the outsourcing of things like cleaning and check-in.

- *MashVisor (https://www.mashvisor.com/)* A web-based information service for real-estate investors.

- *PriceLabs (http://PriceLabs)* An on-line service which automatically updates the price of your Airbnb rental to the optimum level.

- *Smartbnb (https://smartbnb.io/)* A web-based service which allows the automation of a number of Airbnb functions.

- *Wheelhouse (https://www.usewheelhouse.com/)* A dynamic pricing tool for Airbnb hosts.

- *Yourwelcome (https://www.yourwelcome.com/)* A rental property app for guests which provides information about local attraction and events.

HOW TO WRITE A GREAT GUEST REVIEW

You will have the opportunity to review your guests on Airbnb. If you were happy with your guests, there shouldn't be a problem. Create a template for a standard positive review in a word-processing application such as Microsoft Word and save it there.

The main thing you are doing in a guest review is telling other Airbnb hosts whether they should be happy to consider this potential guest. You don't have to go into great details – the most helpful reviews are short. The main point is whether you would be happy to host this guest again.

As noted previously, a good message might be something like;

> 'Great guest(s), good communications, respected my house rules and a pleasure to host. I would be delighted to host this guest/these guests again and I would recommend them to any other Airbnb host without reservation.'

To make this more personal, include the guest's first names in the review or add a personal detail about their stay. To save even more time, some Airbnb tools will allow you to create automated, generic guest reviews – these are covered later in this chapter.

Things get a little more complicated if your guest review is negative. If you give a guest a very negative review, it is possible that no other Airbnb host will want to accommodate them. From Airbnb's point of view, this means that they have lost a potential customer. Hosts have reported that negative reviews of guests have been removed by Airbnb due to a claimed breach of the review guidelines or some other technicality far more frequently than positive reviews.

You have three options if you weren't happy with your guests;

- You may choose not to give them a review at all, or,

- You can give a very brief review that mentions some positive aspect of their visit but nothing else. If your review reads only *'Checked-in on time'* that won't breach Airbnb guidelines, but any savvy host will understand that you weren't entirely happy with the totality of their stay, or,

8. Useful tools and Bonus Content

- You can tell it as you see it and accept that Airbnb may decide to remove the review.

You won't be penalized if you post a negative review of a guest and it is later removed by Airbnb.

Free tool available:

www.theairbnbplaybook.com/tools

HOW TO IMPROVE YOUR GUESTS' EXPERIENCE
ENGAGING WITH YOUR GUESTS

When you meet with your guests at check-in and check-out time, make sure you know their names and greet them by name. Offer to share any useful local knowledge about the area and tips on the best local amenities and show an interest in their trip.

WELCOME PACKS

One of the reasons that people choose to stay at an Airbnb rather than a hotel is that they can benefit from the knowledge of a local person. Reinforce this by providing a welcome pack that, in addition to your contact information and things like the Wi-Fi password, contains brochures and publicity materials for local attractions and amenities you have experienced.

Do you have a great local coffee shop or restaurant? Include a menu and directions. Are you close to a spectacular hiking trail? Provide directions and information. Does someone in the area rent out bicycles? Provide a brochure and/or directions. Are you close to public transportation? Provide timetables and directions to the closest access point.

Take time out to think about the sort of information that you would appreciate as a guest and take the effort to include it in a welcome pack.

COMPLIMENTARY ITEMS

Everyone likes something for free. Providing soap, shampoo, conditioner and even things like chocolates, free beverages or even fresh flowers for your guests needn't be expensive, especially if you buy in bulk, but these small gestures matter to your guests.

You can go further, by providing snacks such as nuts or cookies and basic things like bread, milk and cereals. These are all things that will make a weary guest who wants a cup of coffee but can't face going to the store on their first night happy and happy guests mean good reviews.

ENTERTAINMENT

In addition to a television with access to an entertainment service such as Netflix, HBO, etc., consider providing games and books for your guests. Amongst your books, consider providing a travel guide to the local area or city.

LISTEN TO YOUR GUESTS

The reviews that your guests provide give you the most important data about what they do and don't like. This is invaluable information for you as a host – use it to emphasize what guests like and remove or mitigate what they don't.

BECOME AN AIRBNB GUEST YOURSELF

Why not use Airbnb for your own business or leisure travel to find out what the process feels like for a guest. Are there things that you like at the places you stay? Can you incorporate these ideas into your own property? Are there things you didn't like? Can you find ways to avoid these for your own guests?

SLOW SEASON STRATEGIES

Virtually every property rented on Airbnb will have a *'slow season'* – a period when bookings are likely to drop off either because of the weather or a lack of events. However, there are things you can do to attract bookings even during quiet periods.

8. Useful tools and Bonus Content

DISCOUNTS

When you set your Airbnb rental price, you checked your competitors' prices. This is something you should continue to do throughout the year. Are there price fluctuations? This may indicate that your competitors are aware of a slow period and you may also want to drop your prices during this time. Hotels offer a discount of anything up to 40% during the slow season, so you may want to do something similar. Just make sure that your reduced charge still covers your expenses. You can also consider offering larger discounts for weekly and monthly bookings.

If you offer a discount during certain periods, consider updating your listing title during this time to include something like *'New 20% Discount!'* at the beginning of your title. This will help to catch the eye of anyone browsing bookings but don't forget to remove this text when you go back to your regular price.

REMOVE THE EXTRA PERSON CHARGE

Some Airbnb rentals add an extra charge when you have more than a certain number of guests. Some make an extra person charge if you bring a pet. Consider dropping these during the slow season.

GO FOR A ONE-NIGHT MINIMUM STAY

If you haven't already set one night as the minimum length of stay you accept, consider doing this during the slow season.

TURN ON INSTANT BOOKING

If you haven't already selected the Instant Booking option, the slow season is a good time to try this – it may bring in a few extra bookings.

EXTEND YOUR CALENDAR AVAILABILITY

Before the slow season begins, adjust your calendar so that it shows the period of the slow season and into the next demand period. That way, potential guests can see just how much your rate drops during the slow season, and this may help to encourage bookings.

TWEAK YOUR HOUSE RULES

Do your house rules say no to pets? Perhaps this is something you might want to reconsider during the slow season. Are there any other restrictions in your House Rules that you might be willing to reconsider during certain periods?

CREATE ADDITIONAL REVENUE STREAMS

There are a number of ways to add additional revue streams to supplement your Airbnb rental income.

TRANSPORT

Offer a transport service to collect guests from and/or take them to your local airport/bus/rail station. Many guests will appreciate the ease and security of being collected after a journey. Just make sure you clarify the price first and ensure that your motor insurance covers you for paid journeys.

CHARGE EXTRA FOR EARLY/LATE CHECK-IN

Your check-in time will be noted in your listing, but if a guest plans to arrive outside this time, you can make a small additional charge as long as this is made clear in advance.

OFFER ADDITIONAL SERVICES

You can offer your guests additional services such as laundry or dry-cleaning and either do these yourself or find a local supplier. Make the price clear to the guest beforehand and include a margin to cover your time.

EARN COMMISSION ON LOCAL ACTIVITIES

If there are local amenities and/or events in your area, talk to the proprietors and ask if they will give you a referral commission for every guest you send to them. Don't go for well-known attractions – guests will likely already know about them. Focus on small, less known activities that are unique to your area.

8. Useful tools and Bonus Content

RENT OUT BICYCLES OR OTHER ITEMS

Some Airbnb hosts provide things like bicycles to guests free of charge, and that's a nice extra. However, you can consider renting these things out instead – just make sure that anything you rent out is in good condition and that guests understand that an additional charge will apply.

ADD REFERRAL CODES TO YOUR LISTING

Some services such as Uber and Lyft offer the option to use referral codes. If guests use these, they get a small discount and you get a small commission. Add these to your listing.

GET CREATIVE!

Do you paint or produce ceramics or other artwork? Display a few of these in your property and let guests know they're for sale – these items can make great souvenirs for guests. If you don't produce your own artwork, is there a local artist who does and who might appreciate additional exposure? Add brochures for their work or artworks to your property and negotiate a sales commission with the artist.

AUTOMATING YOUR AIRBNB BUSINESS
AUTOMATED PRICING

Many factors can impact your optimum rental charge including seasonal changes or large events. Ideally, you want to monitor changing conditions to ensure that you always have the optimum price. However, that's a time-consuming process. Automating this within Airbnb is possible using the *Smart Pricing* feature but, as previously noted, many hosts feel that this results in unrealistically low prices. However, there are also third-party solutions which can help.

We have already discussed *Beyond Pricing, AirGMS* and *PriceLabs* which all support dynamic pricing. However, these are fairly complex tools which do much more than just monitor and adjust the price of your rental. There are other simpler solutions which are aimed principally at ensuring that the rental charge for your property is always at the optimum level.

One of the most popular pricing tools previously used by Airbnb hosts was *Everbooked*, but unfortunately this service is no longer available, having been bought over and integrated into the management service offered by *Evolve (https://evolvevacationrental.com/)*. However, there is a new service available, *Wheelhouse (https://www.usewheelhouse.com/)*, created by one of the founders of *Beyond Pricing* and now operating in competition with that product. Wheelhouse analyses billions of data points to assess the optimum rental charge for your property and automatically applies this.

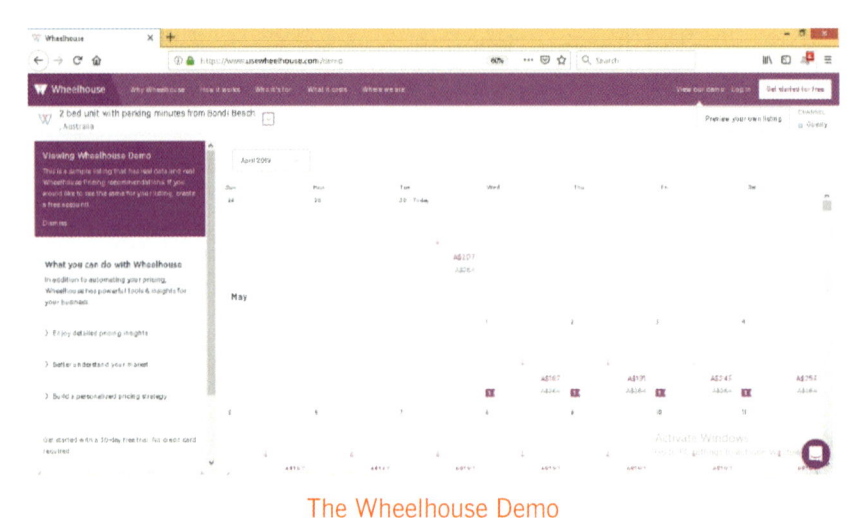

The Wheelhouse Demo
Available at https://www.usewheelhouse.com/demo

There is no doubt that using some form of automated dynamic pricing tool will keep your Airbnb income as high as possible. The Airbnb Smart Pricing feature can help, but it does seem to set prices very low – after all, Airbnb want to attract customers. Other dynamic pricing tools such as Beyond Pricing, Wheelhouse and others seem to take a more objective view and produce more realistic price suggestions.

Some of these products, Wheelhouse for example, offer a free three-month trial, so you can try this out to see if it produces the results you want.

However, you choose to control it, your Airbnb rental charge isn't something that you can *'set and forget'* if you want to optimize your income. Whether you

8. Useful tools and Bonus Content

do it manually or by using a specialist tool, you do need to continually review your Airbnb rental charge.

AUTOMATED MESSAGING

Unfortunately, there is very little automation available within Airbnb messaging though, as described earlier, you can purchase third-party apps and services which will do this. If you don't want to use one of these third-party services, you will have to manually respond to each message and booking request. You can speed up this process by creating generic responses where these are applicable and saving these in MS Word or similar and then copying and pasting the text into your Airbnb messages. Depending on the length of stay, these can include;

- **Booking confirmation.** Sent as soon as the booking is confirmed. Thanking your guest for booking and providing your full address and a guide to travel, parking and anything else the guest is likely to need before arrival.

- **Check-in reminder.** Sent 24 – 48 hours before your guests are due to arrive. Contains confirmation of check-in time and procedures.

- **Welcome message.** Sent 24 hours after the guest(s) arrive. Welcoming them to your property and checking that everything is as expected.

- **Check-out reminder.** Sent on the guests' last evening in your property. Confirms check-out time and procedures.

- **Review Reminder.** Sent within 24 hours of the guests leaving. Asking them to provide a review of your property and reminding them of the importance of 5 Star reviews.

Preparing these messages ahead of time will speed up your responses, but it still doesn't provide automation. If you want to be able to set standard responses which will be sent automatically in certain circumstances, you will need to use a third-party application.

Some of the Airbnb tools already discussed, AirGMS for example, provide facilities to enable automated response to messages. Other tools are designed mainly to support automated messaging.

One of the most popular message automation systems for Airbnb hosts is *Smartbnb (https://smartbnb.io/)*. This solution allows the automation of virtually every message you are likely to send as an Airbnb host, from responses to booking enquiries to check-in and check-out reminders and review reminders. It even allows you to automate your review of guests, randomly selecting review text from several templates you can upload.

The Smartbnb Dashboard
Image from https://smartbnb.io/

Another option is to use a dedicated property management software such as *Guesty (https://www.guesty.com/)*. This also allows the automation of several messaging tasks for hosts but it also gives you access to a dedicated team of people who will respond to messages on your behalf.

8. Useful tools and Bonus Content

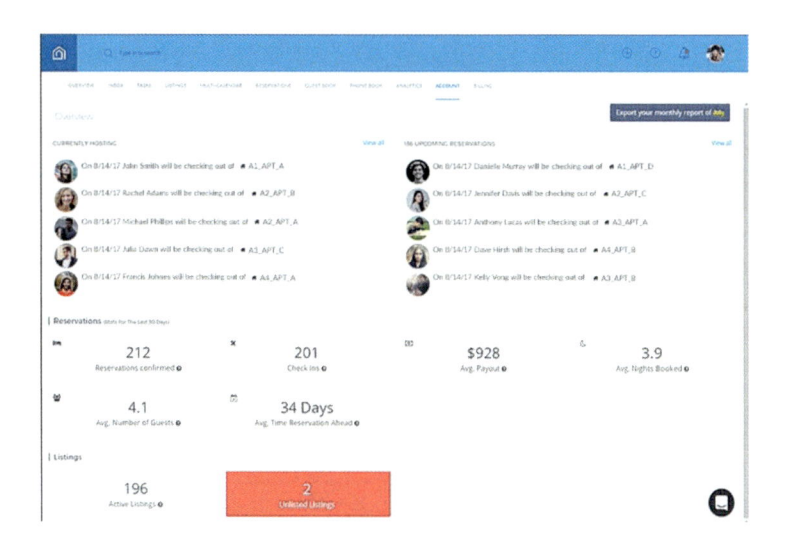

Part of the Guesty Dashboard
Image from https://www.guesty.com/

If your Airbnb business is a success, you will spend a lot of time responding to messages. Automation is a great way of reducing the amount of time you need to spend on this, but the specialist tools described above will cost which will cut into your bottom line. As with many aspects of being an Airbnb host, whether you decide to use one of these all depends on how much time you have available.

AIRBNB HOST ASSIST PROGRAM

Launched in 2015, the Airbnb *Host Assist Program* is a collection of Airbnb approved external services for hosts. These are only available in certain geographical areas – to check if your listing is covered, log into your Airbnb account and navigate to the *Host Assist* section of your dashboard.

The *Host Assist Program* identifies suitable external suppliers in three areas:

- **Physical key handover.** Includes services such as *KeyCafe (https://www.hoardspot.com/en)* and *Hoard (https://www.hoardspot.com/en)* which allows keys to be deposited with trusted local partners and collected by your guests.

- **Keyless and remote access.** Includes services such as *RemoteLock (https://www.igloohome.co/)* and *IglooHome (https://www.igloohome.co/)* which allow access to your property for guests without the need for you to be on-site.

- **Cleaning services.** Includes cleaning service providers such as *Properly (https://www.getproperly.com/en)*.

For many of these services, Airbnb have negotiated discounts for Airbnb hosts and in some cases, integration with your Airbnb listing.

Many of these services are available only in limited areas so do check what is available in your area under the Host Assist Program by logging in to your Airbnb account.

CONCLUSION

There are many different boxes that need to be ticked to become a successful Airbnb entrepreneur and, when you are just getting started, understanding all the various aspects can seem daunting.

But now you have The Airbnb Playbook and if you follow the step-by-step guidance provided in this book, you will be giving yourself the best chance of succeeding while ensuring that you avoid the most common pitfalls and mistakes that many new hosts make.

Running an Airbnb business isn't that different to running any other form of business. You need to plan carefully using reliable data, understand your market, target demographic and set prices to maximize your profits, and above all else keep your customers satisfied.

Whether you want to generate a little additional income from renting out a spare room or you want to buy multiple properties and become an Airbnb entrepreneur, the sky is the limit if you use the guidelines in this book.

I wish you every success.

I hope you enjoyed reading this book. If you did, please take a moment to leave me a review on Amazon. Your opinion matters and positive reviews help me greatly. Thank you.

I welcome feedback from readers. If you have comments on this book or ideas for other books, please send me an email at theairbnbplaybook@gmail.com

Thanks

James Steward

BONUS CONTENT!!

As a thank you for putting your trust in me and this book I am giving every reader free access to download all the free tools and templates me and my team have created and that helped us succeed on our Airbnb journey.

You can download all the tools and templates here:

www.theairbnbplaybook.com/tools

Please keep this link private and do not redistribute it.
Thank you

James

GLOSSARY

- **ADR** – Average Daily Rate. Also referred to as the **Weighted Daily Average Rate** is derived by taking an average of weekday and weekend rates for all available rooms/apartments/properties.

- **Cash on Cash Return.** A metric used to evaluate the revenue return on income-producing assets. Expressed as a percentage derived by dividing the annual before-tax cash flow by the total amount of money invested.

- **KPI** – Key Performance Indicator. Any quantifiable measurement used to measure progress towards operational or strategic goals.

- **Occupancy Rate** – A standard KPI used by the hospitality industry. Derived by calculating the average percentage of available rental space which is occupied during a defined period.

- **RevPAR** – Revenue Per Available Room. Another standard metric used as a Key Performance Indicator (KPI) in the hospitality industry. Derived by multiplying the ADR of all available rooms by the average Occupancy Rate.

🌐 INDEX OF LINKS 🌐

1. Airbnb Cancellation Policies; https://www.airbnb.com/home/cancellation_policies#strict-with-grace-period
2. Airbnb Collections; https://www.airbnb.com/help/article/2185/what-is-a-collection?
3. Airbnb Family Collection; https://www.airbnb.com/help/article/2187/how-do-i-join-the-family-collection?
4. Airbnb Help Center; https://www.airbnb.com/help/
5. Airbnb Help Center Article *'Responsible hosting in the United States'*; https://www.airbnb.com/help/article/1376/responsible-hosting-in-the-united-states
6. Airbnb Neighborhoods; https://www.airbnb.com/locations
7. Airbnb Plus checklist; https://www.airbnb.com/b/plushomechecklist
8. Airbnb Review Content Guidelines; https://www.airbnb.com/help/article/546/what-is-airbnb-s-content-policy
9. Airbnb Work Collection; https://www.airbnb.com/help/article/2186/how-do-i-join-the-work-collection?
10. AirDNA; https://www.airdna.co/
11. AirDNA Rentalizer; https://www.airdna.co/vacation-rental-valuation
12. AirGMS; https://www.airgms.com/
13. Beyond Pricing; https://beyondpricing.com/
14. Evolve; https://evolvevacationrental.com/
15. Guest Ready; https://www.guestready.com/
16. Guesty; https://www.guesty.com/

17. Hoard; https://www.hoardspot.com/en

18. HostMaker; https://hostmaker.com/

19. IglooHome; *https://www.igloohome.co/*

20. KeyCafe; https://www.keycafe.com/

21. MashVisor; https://www.mashvisor.com

22. Mister Suite; https://www.mistersuite.com/

23. My VR Host; https://www.myvrhost.com/

24. Pillow; https://www.pillow.com/

25. Piper Home Security; https://getpiper.com/

26. PriceLabs; https://pricelabs.co/

27. Properly; https://www.getproperly.com/en

28. RemoteLock; https://www.remotelock.com/

29. Rented.com; https://www.rented.com/

30. Sharing or embedding an Airbnb listing on another site; https://www.airbnb.com/help/article/923/how-can-i-share-or-embed-my-listing-on-other-websites

31. Smartbnb; https://smartbnb.io/

32. Vacasa; https://www.vacasa.com/

33. Wheelhouse; https://www.usewheelhouse.com/

34. Yourwelcome; https://www.yourwelcome.com/

Free tool available:

www.theairbnbplaybook.com/tools

INDEX

Airbnb Plus	80,87
AirDNA	18,19,20,23,27,28,42,119
AirGMS	29,119,125,127
Beyond Pricing	24,25,26,27,28,119,125,126
Brian Chesky	7,8
Business Plan	15,16,18,35,37,38,46,47
Calendar	22,26,74,76,85,89,123
Cancellation	72,73,85,87,97,99
Cleaning	2,11,28,50,57,62,77,82,90,91,100,107,108,109, 110,111,112,113,114,119,124,130
Cleaning fee	77
Goals	1,13,14,38,77
Guesty	112,119,128,129
Host Assist Program	129,130
Host Guarantee	47,48,49,95
Host Protection	47,48,49
Instant Book	10,75,76,85,95
Insurance	2,15,28,31,37,41,42,47,48,49,51,108,124
Joe Gebbia	7,8
MashVisor	20,21,42,119
Nathan Blecharczyk	7,8,58
Occupancy Rate	16,18,24,27,43,53,76,86,90,111
One night minimum	10,75,77
Pets	31,62,63,64,72,76,124
Price	22,24,25,26,27,44,46,49,73,77,78,119,123,124, 125,126
PriceLabs	24,26,27,28,119,125

Regulations	33,34,35,41,42,44,45,49
Rental arbitrage	4,42,43,45,51
Review	2,10,11,30,50,73,78,84,85,90,92,93,94,96,97,98, 99,100,102,103,104,120,121,126,127,128
Safety	9,10,30,32,61
SEO	10,84,87
Smartbnb	119,128
Strata	35,41,44,51
Superhost	75,78,79,87,89,97,102
Target Demographic	14,23,24,54,67,69,81
Tax	28,33,34,36,37,45,59
Trends	21,22,27
Wheelhouse	119,126
Yourwelcome	60,119

Made in the USA
Middletown, DE
24 January 2021